# Green Kitchen Travels

DAVID FRENKIEL & LUISE VINDAHL

# Green Kitchen
# Travels

hardie grant books

MELBOURNE · LONDON

To Elsa.

During these first 4 years of your life, you have followed us to 15 different countries and 5 continents. In a couple of wild months back in 2010, we slept in new cities and different beds almost every day and bounced back and forth across the time zones. It wouldn't have been strange if you had cried and complained through this, but instead you have been laughing, sleeping and eating your way around the world and faced every new destination with wide-open eyes.

If you had been any different, these pages would never have been written.

We love you.

# Contents

# Introduction

'Hey Ali Baba, come and try this yoghurt!' A Moroccan teenager is waving enthusiastically at me. He must have seen how curiously I am looking at the large gathering of young and old people, all standing with bowls filled to the brim with something gloppy and pink. An old man with a big straw hat is scooping up the runny strawberry yoghurt from plastic containers balanced on his wobbly cart, next to a bowl with hot water to quickly wash up the bowls for new customers. I glance at the plastic containers, the gloppy yoghurt, the half-cleaned bowls and then at Luise. 'You know you want to,' she encourages me. 'I know. I do. It's just that if I were a nasty bacteria I would probably thrive in that yoghurt.' The teenager sees my hesitation. 'Come now Ali Baba, you must try this. It is THE BEST!' I smile, ask my stomach for forgiveness and step forward to grab a bowl. 'Fill it up!'

Whether we are trying sweet, gloppy yoghurts in the Moroccan Medina, falling asleep to the never-ending noise from the New York City streets or waking up to the sound of crashing waves in a small bungalow in Sri Lanka, our little family has always felt most at home when we are not. There are so many unexplored places to see, interesting people to meet, stories to hear and new food to be tried.

I suppose the fact that I am Swedish, Luise is Danish and we met in Italy was a good indication how impossible it would be for us to stay in one country. Luckily we both shared the same love of travelling. After our daughter Elsa was born, it only took a few months before we flew back to Italy to spend a summer month. When she was seven months old, we took a break from our jobs in Stockholm and went on a journey together around the world. We slept on a friend's couch in Brooklyn, USA; rented a car and drove down the amazing Highway 1 from San Francisco to San Diego; tried to find someone who could guide us to a vegetarian restaurant in Beijing (not the easiest task) and were mesmerised by the street vendors in Vietnam and the lemongrass-filled curries in Thailand. By the time we came back to Sweden, we had emptied every penny from our savings but filled our passports with stamps, our hearts with inspiration and our stomachs with delicious food.

And somehow, on a small island outside Vietnam, Elsa had also learned how to walk.

Not all our travels are as high-flying. Sometimes it's just a drive to friends outside Stockholm; a train ride to Denmark; a boat trip around Greece; or a bike ride in Barcelona. We are mostly drawn towards warmer countries, probably to make up for the dark and cold autumns and winters here in Scandinavia.

Regardless of destination, the food has always been the most exciting adventure for us. Visiting green markets, trying regional vegetarian specialities and figuring out how to get invited into the locals' kitchens are top of our 'to do' list when arriving at new places. It might seem a little nerdy, but we love learning how ingredients such as lentils can be cooked for dinner in the US and for dessert in Asia. How similar (and yet so different) an Italian focaccia is to an Indian naan. And how adding a little cinnamon, cumin and raisins to a French ratatouille suddenly gives it a Moroccan twist.

Food truly is a language on its own and has opened doors and connected us with many fantastic people whom we never would have met otherwise: the old couple (he had been a vegetarian for 75 years!) we ended up having dinner with at our favourite café in Barcelona, the avocado-orchard family in California who invited us for lunch and showed us how to pick ripe avocados fresh from the trees (while managing not to step on the rattlesnakes!), and the pretty lady boy chef in Thailand with painted nails who taught us how to make green curries, coconut soups and pomelo salads. Even though cultures, ingredients, methods and flavours may be very different around the world, the people who are genuinely interested in food seem to have a special connection and are always the friendliest in town. Food is not only our favourite part of a trip; it is also what we bring with us back home. When memories fade away and our skin turns pale again, we keep our adventures alive in our Stockholm kitchen. Herbs, flavours and scents bring back more vivid images than any photo ever could.

All of our inspiration, experiences and random food encounters are gathered in this cookery book. – *David*

# Food Philosophy

In our first book, *The Green Kitchen* (UK edition)/*Vegetarian Everyday* (US edition), we explained in detail the thoughts behind our way of eating, so we won't bore you with too much of that here. But in order to explain why the recipes in this book are different from many other travel-inspired cookery books, we wanted to give you a quick recap.

Our approach to food and cooking can best be explained as healthy, natural and green. It is food that is centred around vegetables, good fats, natural sweeteners, whole grains, legumes, seeds, nuts and fruit. Our cooking methods focus on maximizing natural flavours instead of destroying the nutrients.

Eating is not a science to us. We simply focus on good, whole foods rather than highly processed ones. We use good-quality produce, organic when possible and not genetically modified, and we try to eat as varied a diet as possible. Many of our recipes

happen to be vegan, even though we are not. And almost all the recipes in this book are naturally gluten-free, although we do sometimes bake with spelt, rye or other whole grains. We want to feel strengthened and energized after a dinner, not heavy and bloated.

We have learned that the best way of eating well is not by forbidding ingredients. Instead, we try to have a balanced approach to food. Listening to our bodies' needs makes more sense than setting up rules for what we can or cannot eat. We wouldn't travel to Rome without eating a few cones of gelato or visit a market in Udaipur, India, without trying some of the oily fried pakoras or other chaat (street food). But we also make sure to dive into countries' natural treats, such as Sri Lankan pineapples, fresh Thai coconuts, Sicilian oranges, California strawberries and Moroccan dates.

KEEP
CALM
FRESH
FRUIT
JUICE
AVAILABLE

*GUACAMOLE                    45
*NACHOS                      100
*BEEF NACHOS                 150
*SHRIMP CEVICHE              180
*CONCH CEVICHE               180
*MIXED CEVICHE

SPECIAL
TODAY
JalaPeños
o PePPers
1 dummy!

*BIG GRILLED SHRIMP          200
**GRILLED FISH FILLET        180
**GRILLED CONCH FILLET       200
*GRILLED CHEESE BURGER       100
*GRILLED FISH

# Locality, Recipes & Methods

Most of the recipes in this book are inspired by the trips we have made together as a family during these last four years, but we have also included a few from earlier travels. You will find references to Spain, Portugal, Italy, Greece, USA, Mexico, Morocco, India, Sri Lanka, Bali, Thailand, Vietnam and China. There are some recipes from Denmark and even one from Sweden. We have also included a couple of recipes that we find useful in transit and when coming home.

There are endless numbers of great cookery books focused on traditional local cuisines, many of the best ones written by locals. It has never been our intention to cover that area. The recipes in this book are influenced by the countries we have visited, but they are to a much greater degree a reflection of us. They are based on the people we have met, the food we have tried and the ingredients we have come across and then adapted to our preferences, cooking habits and style to make them our own.

If the original recipes called for deep-frying, sugar-drenching or gluten, we have changed the cooking method, replaced the sugar with natural sweeteners and come up with simple gluten-free alternatives. Our Chinese-inspired steamed Mushroom & Tofu Dumplings (page 165) are wrapped in rice paper instead of dumpling dough, which makes them easy to prepare, gluten-free and amazingly tasty. We try other variations, too; the delicious North African marinade chermoula is normally used on fish, but in our kitchen we rub it into a cauliflower that we oven-bake whole – the spices spread a wonderful scent through the kitchen (page 149). And some recipes need no adjusting at all – the Mexican Paletas (page 204) that look almost too good to be true are surprisingly uncomplicated, naturally sweet and full of flavour, so they suit our repertoire perfectly.

Just because we love to travel, it doesn't mean that you have to. We have adapted all the recipes to what we can find in the stores around the area where we live. You might need to visit an Asian market for a handful of the recipes, but the large part of them can be prepared with simple ingredients that you will find in your local supermarket.

The book is divided into traditional chapters to make it easier to navigate in everyday cooking. We have organized the recipes based on how we prefer to eat at home. The Breakfast chapter has a fabulous mix of sweet and savoury dishes. The Street Food & Snacks chapter will hopefully be handy when you are throwing a party. The Soup chapter has some great soups for cold days (and a chilled avocado soup for hot days). The Salad & Sides chapter shows how very different accompaniments can be, depending on their origin. The Dinner chapter has both quick meals for a stressed Tuesday evenings and more elaborate projects for a Saturday night family gathering, and Drips & Drops has a whole selection of hot and cold drinks. And we have, of course, included a delicious Desserts chapter with some of our favourite sweet treats from around the world.

We have also added a chapter to share our best tips for travelling with kids. It's a compilation of all the small things that we have found helpful on our trips around the world with our daughter, Elsa.

Most of the recipes were written for this book, but we have included a few favourites from our blog. They have new photos and many of them have also been altered in different ways – new flavours have been added, the way of preparing some of them has been perfected, or new serving suggestions have been dreamt up. So even though you might think you've seen a recipe before, it might be worth trying it again. These are all dishes that we love and cook often. They remind us how travelling the world has brought many new and unexpected pleasures to our kitchen – and we hope they will now also find their way into your homes too.

Have fun!

# Travelling
# with Kids

After taking our daughter on trains, boats and planes across five continents, we have learned a few tricks on how to keep her happy, calm and safe. Travelling with kids or a baby definitely has its challenging moments but with some basic planning, lots of love and by putting your baby's needs first, you will end up having an amazing trip.

When we started our adventures, Elsa was three months old. She was having breast milk only, but after a couple of months started to eat small portions of solid food, such as mild vegetable purées with cold-pressed oils or butter. During our journey around the world, she progressed to an entirely solid diet, similar to ours. We know how personal the subject of breast versus bottle is – and all mothers must do what works best for them – but we can tell you that in those early months of travelling, it was definitely convenient not to have to think about her food.

The tips we have gathered here have worked for us. Kids are different and even if all of these tips might not work for you, hopefully a few of them will come in handy.

## PACKING

### 1. Can it fit in a tuc-tuc?

If you plan to stay in more than one place during your trip, you will do yourself a big favour by not bringing all the baby equipment and toys from home. It is also a liberating feeling, realising that you don't need all those things. Keep in mind that it's not just about the baggage allowance on a plane – you should also be able to fit all your luggage into a taxi, boat, or sometimes even a tiny tuc-tuc (although we have learned that most drivers can squeeze almost anything into this three-wheeler).

Apart from baby clothes, pacifiers, nappies, a few plastic bags, bottles and other obvious stuff, here are a few things that we found useful on our trip:

• A baby carrier. Preferably one that you can also use on your back – we love our Ergo.

• A lightweight folding pushchair. Make sure it can recline completely so your baby can sleep in it – we have found a Chicco Liteway suits our needs.

• A portable fabric baby chair. This is a great little invention that you can mount to any chair and then fold up and fit into your pocket. It was good to have one on hand before Elsa could sit properly by herself. Check out the Swedish-designed In The Pocket Baby or the British Totseat, both available online.

• A baby monitor. This gives you peace of mind so you can relax while your baby is napping. There are also a few great phone apps that you can use.

• A mosquito net. Some bungalows and hotels already have mosquito nets, but far from all, so it's a good idea to have your own. We had one big net that we put over our bed, and a small net that we put over Elsa's stroller. They take up little or no space and can really save the night.

• Instant organic gluten-free porridge. We used porridge as emergency food whenever we needed to give Elsa something quick without having to find a restaurant. You can buy porridge in larger supermarkets all around the world, but it's hard to find the unsweetened instant kind. If it comes in a box, pack it in a plastic sealable bag instead – it takes up less space.

### 2. Just in case

Make sure that you know whom to call if your baby (or you) becomes ill. A good tip is to take the contact details for your GP and health visitor with you so that you may be able to discuss health concerns with them without worrying about language difficulties and possible misunderstandings. In case of emergencies, it's also worth checking out before you travel where hospitals and other

medical services are to be found wherever you are staying in the world, and your nearest embassy, too.

We also created a small natural travel pharmacy that helped us many times through our trip. If you are more into traditional medicine, you can probably find equivalent things in most pharmacies.

- Homeopathic remedies to ease the symptoms of flu, colds, fevers and minor infections.
- Probiotic drops or powder to boost digestive and immune systems.
- Homeopathic cream to relieve pain and skin problems, bites, rashes and so on. We use products from Heel, but everyone has their favourites.
- Rescue Remedy Cream from Bach Flower Remedies (for skin problems, wounds, bites, rashes and so on).
- Herbal pain relief spray (we use Spenglersan).
- Citronella oil spray as a non-toxic mosquito remedy. Where mosquitoes are numerous, we spray Elsa's clothes the evening before she wears them.
- Mini first aid kit.
- Relief of fever suspension drops.
- Oral rehydration salts.
- Sea band bracelets for children to prevent motion sickness.

## ON THE PLANE

### 3. Have a bottle ready

If you don't breast-feed, always have a bottle with formula or water with you when you get on an aeroplane. Let your baby drink during take-offs and landings to help prevent inner ear pain.

### 4. New toys on the plane

You know how it always takes at least 30 minutes of waiting on the plane before take-off? These minutes can be quite challenging for parents, since babies normally don't like to sit still with the seatbelt on. For those occasions we sometimes bring tiny new toys (or download new apps now that Elsa is older), that we don't show her until we are on the plane. Opening the wrappings and playing with them usually keeps her occupied and sitting still during that time. When we arrive at a new destination she often chooses to give the toys to kids living there, so we don't have to carry new toys from destination to destination. The same thing goes for beach toys.

### 5. Don't run out of snacks

Bring lots of snacks (fruit, hard-boiled eggs, instant porridge, vegetable smoothies, gluten-free crackers, raw food bars, avocado, carrots, sprouts and so on). Giving babies and small children a snack is always a good trick to prevent them starting to scream with hunger. We have found ourselves in too many unexpected situations (such as traffic jams) with a hungry and screaming Elsa. It's not fun, but can easily be avoided. Nowadays we never leave home without emergency snacks in our bag.

## ACCOMMODATION

### 6. Be picky about your place

When you have a baby, you will spend more time in your hotel room, house or bungalow than you think, so make sure that you choose a place where you feel comfortable. If you are on a beach holiday, it might be worth finding a beach-front location. That way you can dip your toes in the ocean and relax in the sun while the baby sleeps in the shade where you can see her. If you want to keep the cost down, consider home exchange. By swapping with other families, you will get a home suited to kids. We have used homeexchange.com with great success. Airbnb.com is also a good source for finding accommodation around the world and keeping the living costs down.

### 7. Keep them close

If you move around to lots of different locations, your child might feel a little insecure. Always show her around when you arrive at a new place, and if she has trouble sleeping, let her sleep in your bed. That way she will always feel safe, no matter where in the world you are.

## EATING

### 8. Skip the menu

Even in the most remote places in the world we found children's menus in the restaurants, but since we don't feed Elsa meat or overly processed food, we rarely found anything decent on them. Our best advice is to talk to the waiter or the chef (if they speak English) and explain what your baby/toddler likes. They can almost always fix some yummy wholefood, even if it is not on the menu.

### 9. Eat early ... or late

Bringing a small baby to a restaurant doesn't have to mean trouble – just do it on their terms. Even though it might feel a little awkward having dinner around 5–6 pm, in a half-empty restaurant, that is usually your best chance of having a no-cry dinner. You don't have to wait for the food, plus there is lots of space for playing. If you prefer to eat late, give your baby something to eat at home then put her in the stroller at the regular sleeping time and hopefully she'll fall asleep on the way to the restaurant so you can enjoy a quiet and romantic dinner.

### 10. Try the local luxuries

If your baby eats solid food, let her try the wonderful fresh produce available, such as fresh coconut, avocados, buckwheat pancakes, miso soup, grilled corn cobs, warm chestnuts, dragon fruit, pomelo, lychees and, maybe, even a wheatgrass shot. That stuff is so much better than baby crackers, bottled juices and bread.

## OTHER

### 11. Take turns

Vacation is about relaxation, but since small babies need a lot of attention, it's not always easy to find the time to read a book or just doze off. We took turns in taking care of Elsa so that the other one could have time of total relaxation.

### 12. Leave your rules at home

Things are different when you travel as you constantly run into challenges that you haven't faced before. Try to be open and ready to adjust to whatever happens. Don't take the view 'This is how we do it at home so this is how it should be', since adapting to circumstances can avoid a lot of argument and worry. Just try to make it clear to your child that you are doing things differently because you are travelling, but when you are home the normal rules apply.

### 13. The best school

On our trips, Elsa has asked us a million questions and made a million observations based on what she has seen: 'Why don't we have hot water here?', 'Why are those men wearing dresses?' and 'Look, Mummy, all the women have scarves on their heads.' Seeing different cultures is a great way for your kids to learn and be more open to all the cultural and religious differences on this planet.

Don't be afraid of what kind of problems you could run into. Travelling is an amazing experience and you will never regret it.

TRAVELLING WITH KIDS

CHAPTER ONE

# BREAKFASTS

# Deluxe Acai Bowl

In Santa Barbara we rented the top floor of a large and lavish house only a few blocks from the beach. After having spent the previous weeks in shabby motels, we felt like a royal family up there. The owner was an artist of some kind and she agreed to let us stay there for a very low rent. Often on our travels, people are surprisingly kind to us. It must be the baby in the pushchair that helps soften their hearts. In a back alley, only a short walk from the house, we found a café where all the cool kids hung out. The café served an array of purple açaí bowls that we soon learned were both delicious and very healthy. After leaving Santa Barbara and continuing down south, we started stocking up on frozen açaí pulp and making our own bowls whenever we had access to a kitchen. In Sweden (and many parts of the world) frozen açaí is both hard to find and very expensive so nowadays we make our bowls with açaí powder and other kinds of frozen berries. It can be found in most health food stores.

*300 g (10½ oz/2 cups) frozen strawberries,*
*slightly thawed*
*2 frozen sliced bananas*
*4 tbsp açai powder*
*about 250 ml (8½ fl oz/1 cup) unsweetened*
*almond milk (or milk of choice)*
*2 tbsp of any of the following: nut or seed butter,*
*plant-based protein powders (made from hemp*
*seeds, brown rice, sprouted peas or seeds), or*
*soaked nuts or seeds*

*Topping*
*fresh fruit, sliced*
*hemp seeds*
*bee pollen*
*goji berries*
*clear honey (preferably unheated), optional*

Place the frozen fruits, açaí powder and milk in a strong high-speed blender. Add the nut butter, protein powder or soaked nuts or seeds, if using. Mix until creamy and smooth. Aim for a frozen yoghurt consistency. If you do not have a strong high-speed blender, use a hand blender and mix in a tall jug. Spoon the açai mixture into bowls and top with sliced fruit, hemp seeds, bee pollen, goji berries and a drizzle of honey, if using. Serve immediately.

# Overnight Soaked Oats

Prepare these jars in the evening, place in the fridge and while you are sleeping, the liquid is soaking the oats so they will be soft, sweet and ready to be eaten at sunrise. They're perfect for busy mornings or when the weather is getting warmer and you want to enjoy breakfast in the park. I have also made this for brunch gatherings where I prepared a lot of small jars filled with different flavours. It looks fun with handwritten stickers on the jars and everyone can choose their favourite one. Soaking grains and seeds makes them easier to digest, the nutrients are more readily absorbed and it gives the oats a silky consistency. The first time we discovered this method was in the restaurant Peels in New York City.

Lucuma powder is made from ground, dried Peruvan lucuma fruit and is a natural sweetener, packed with nutrients. It's available from health food shops and online. — *Luise*

## Basic Recipe

*60 g (2 oz/½ cup) old-fashioned rolled oats*
  *(gluten-free, if intolerant)*
*a pinch of ground sweet spice (vanilla,*
  *cinnamon, cardamom or mixed spice)*
*1 tbsp seeds (chia, flax, sesame, psyllium etc.)*
*175 ml (6 fl oz /¾ cup) unsweetened plant*
  *milk or juice (almond, oat, coconut water*
  *or coconut milk, orange, apple etc.)*

Combine all the dry ingredients in a small glass jar, cover with the chosen liquid, stir to mix and close with a lid. Place in the fridge for a few hours or overnight. It will keep there for 3–5 days.

## Blueberry, Vanilla & Chia

*60 g (2 oz/½ cup) old-fashioned rolled oats*
  *(gluten-free, if intolerant)*
*a pinch of ground vanilla or a few drops of*
  *vanilla extract*
*1 tbsp chia seeds*
*175 ml (6 fl oz/¾ cup) unsweetened*
  *almond milk*
*2 tbsp fresh or frozen blueberries*

Combine the oats, vanilla and chia seeds in a small glass jar, cover with the milk, stir to mix and top with blueberries. Close with a lid and place in the fridge for a few hours or overnight.

# Lucuma & Hazelnut

60 g (2 oz/½ cup) old-fashioned rolled oats
   (gluten-free, if intolerant)
1 tsp sesame seeds
1 tsp lucuma powder
175 ml (6 fl oz/¾ cup) almond milk
1 tbsp hazelnut (filbert) butter

Combine all the dry ingredients in a glass jar. Cover with the milk, stir to mix, and carefully stir in the hazelnut butter. Close with a lid and place in the fridge for a few hours or overnight.

# Raw Cacao, Chia & Banana

60 g (2 oz/½ cup) old-fashioned rolled oats
   (gluten-free, if intolerant)
1 tsp chia seeds
1 tbsp raw cacao or unsweetened cocoa powder
½ banana, mashed
175 ml (6 fl oz/¾ cup) almond milk

Combine all the dry ingredients in a small glass jar. Add the mashed banana and work it into the oat mixture. Cover with the milk, stir to mix and close with a lid. Place in the fridge for a few hours or overnight.

# Peanut butter, Banana & Raspberry

60 g (2 oz/½ cup) old-fashioned rolled oats
   (gluten-free, if intolerant)
175 ml (6 fl oz/¾ cup) almond milk
½ banana, mashed
1 tbsp peanut butter
2 tbsp mashed raspberries or Raw Raspberry
   & Chia Jam (see page 232)

Put the rolled oats in a small glass jar, cover with milk and stir to mix. Carefully stir in the banana and peanut butter and top with the raspberries. Close with a lid. Place in the fridge for a few hours or overnight.

# Orange, Flax & Coconut

2 tbsp flax seeds
60 g (2 oz/½ cup) old-fashioned rolled oats
   (gluten-free, if intolerant)
a pinch of ground vanilla or a few drops
   of vanilla extract
175 ml (6 fl oz/¾ cup) orange juice,
   preferably freshly-squeezed
1 tbsp toasted coconut flakes

Place the flax seeds in a small glass jar. Combine the oats and vanilla and spoon over the flax seeds. Cover with the orange juice and close with a lid. Place in the fridge for a few hours or overnight. Sprinkle toasted coconut flakes on top before serving.

BREAKFASTS

# Mushroom & Spinach Baked Eggs en Cocotte

What I like so much about the French *Oeufs en Cocotte*, or their less romantic-sounding English name Eggs in Pots, is how simple it is to vary the recipe. Sometimes we add kale to the pot, other times we stick to fresh herbs. In France they often add a dash of cream, but a drizzle of almond milk also adds extra richness. The eggs are softly baked on top of the vegetables and when you dip your spoon into the yolk it is supposed to break and integrate with the vegetables in a delicious creamy mess. I remember that the first time I tried this dish, in a café in the Marais district of Paris, it was with mushrooms and spinach, as here. The quantities of mushrooms and spinach need not be precise – but be generous! — *Luise*

*1 tbsp cold-pressed coconut or olive oil, or ghee,*
*plus more to grease the ramekins*
*1 generous handful mushrooms of choice*
*2 generous handfuls fresh spinach,*
*thawed frozen works fine*
*2 sprigs of thyme, finely chopped*
*100 g (3½ oz/½ cup) fresh creamy goats' cheese*
*or sheeps' feta cheese, crumbled*
*2 tbsp pine nuts (pine kernels)*
*4 eggs*
*sea salt and freshly ground pepper*
*a drizzle of cold-pressed olive oil, for serving*

Preheat the oven to 180°C (350°F/Gas 4).

Heat the coconut oil in a frying pan over a medium heat and sauté the mushrooms, spinach and most of the thyme (reserving a little for garnish) for a couple of minutes until soft and tender. Grease the ramekins. Place half the crumbled goats' cheese in the bottom and divide the mushrooms and spinach between the ramekins. Top with the rest of the cheese and the pine nuts. Carefully crack 2 eggs into each dish – you want to keep the egg yolks intact. Season with salt and pepper. Bake in the oven for 10–12 minutes, until the whites are set and the yolks are still soft.

Remove from the oven and add a drizzle of olive oil and a sprinkling of thyme before serving.

# Apple & Oat Scones

'Tomorrow we are going out for brunch,' my friends tell me. It's the same story every time we visit their small but cool Shoreditch apartment. We get to crash on their couch to make the most of our time together (as well as avoiding over-priced London hotels) and in the morning they take us out for long brunches and flower-market visits. One thing we have learned over the years is that Londoners know how to brunch. So far, they have taken us to cool smoothie cafés, greasy burger joints and fun hipster hangouts with ongoing table tennis tournaments. But the most memorable place must have been the bunker-like building with white brick walls, enormously high ceilings and a concert pianist playing – so unexpected! Regardless of the place, we often have a repetitive breakfast pattern; our friends order Bloody Mary and a sandwich, Luise chooses eggs and juice and I always fall for scones (biscuits) and coffee. The scones we bake at home are somewhat different from anything that we have tried in London, being all gluten-free and vegan. But they have the same sweet biscuit quality and can be thrown together in a heartbeat. This version is vegan, but you can replace coconut oil and almond butter with 125 g (4 oz/½ cup) normal butter, if you prefer. — *David*

### Dry Ingredients
200 g (7 oz/1¾ cups) gluten-free oat flour
   (make your own by grinding 3 cups
   gluten-free rolled oats)
150 g (5 oz/1¼ cup) buckwheat flour or
   flour of your choice
1 tbsp arrow root or cornflour (cornstarch)
1 tsp baking powder
½ tsp bicarbonate of soda (baking soda)
1 tsp sea salt

### Wet Ingredients
75 g (2½ oz /5 tbsp) cold-pressed coconut oil
   at room temperature (see note above on butter)
3 tbsp almond butter (or any nut or seed butter
   of your choice)
250 ml (8½ fl oz/1 cup) plain organic, GMO-free soy
   yoghurt (or yoghurt of your choice)
2 eating apples, coarsely grated including the peel
   (you need about 175 g/6 oz/1¼ cups), gently
   squeeze out the excess juice

Preheat the oven to 450°F (230°C/Gas 8) and place a baking sheet inside. Mix together the dry ingredients in a large bowl. Cut the coconut oil into small cubes and add to the flour mixture together with the almond butter. Rub in with the fingertips until the mixture resembles breadcrumbs.

Add the soy yoghurt and apples and mix with a wooden spoon until you can work the dough by hand. It can be slightly crumbly but should come together as you draw it together – try not to over-knead or the scones will turn out hard. If the dough feels too dry, add a dash more yoghurt; if too wet, a little more flour. Flatten out the ball on a floured surface to a 25 cm (10 in) round, about 2.5 cm (1 in) thick. Use a 7.5 cm (3 in) biscuit cutter or glass to cut out as many scones as you can, reshaping and cutting the trimmings as necessary. Cover the hot baking sheet with baking parchment and place the scones on it. Bake for 15–16 minutes or until crusty on the outside and slightly moist on the inside. Slice the scones in half and spread on some fruit compôte or homemade marmalade in between the 2 halves. Eat while still hot. Nothing tastes like these freshly baked.

# Marrakech Orange Blossom & Cardamom Yoghurt

Most cafés and street vendors in Marrakech take pride in making their own raib (yoghurt). It is often rather sweet and spiked with orange blossom water or rose water, which gives it a unique Moroccan flavour. We included a simple recipe for making yoghurt in our last book and have therefore just shared a method for flavouring it here. If you are using bought yoghurt, choose a good-quality full-fat one. Goat or plant-based ones also work great.

*450 ml (15 fl oz/2 cups) plain full-fat yoghurt,*
*    preferably with active live-cultures*
*2 tsp orange blossom water or rose water*
*2 tsp clear honey, (preferably unheated)*
*¼ tsp ground cardamom*

*To Serve*
*fresh fruit*

Put the yoghurt in a bowl. Start with 1 teaspoon of flower water and add with the honey and cardamom. Taste and add more flower water if desired. Divide into 2 jars or glasses, top with fresh fruit and add straws.

Serve immediately.

# Amaranth Porridge with Caramelized Plums

I am pretty sure that we could write a whole book about porridge. We eat various kinds for breakfast almost every day of the week and the possibilities and variations are endless. The buckwheat porridge in our first book is one of our favourites, but when we crave something creamier, this amaranth porridge is one of our go-to options. Before visiting Mexico, we had hardly ever used amaranth in cooking, but there they use it in a million different ways and have inspired us to do the same. The popular amaranth seed can be found in the smallest of stores in Mexico. It has a lot of similarities to its Peruvian cousin quinoa. They contain all essential amino acids and are gluten-free, which makes them even greater for vegans and vegetarians. In Europe you usually find them in health food stores or the special food section at larger supermarkets. If you can't find amaranth you can replace it with quinoa in this recipe. Warm caramelized plums are our favourite topping for weekend mornings. If they are not in season they can be replaced with apples, pears or peaches. — *Luise*

150 g (5 oz/1 cup) amaranth seeds
a pinch of fine sea salt
500 ml (17 fl oz/2 cups) water
120 ml (4 fl oz/½ cup) unsweetened almond milk
4 tbsp unsweetened coconut flakes
½ tsp ground cinnamon

*Warm Caramelized Plums*
1 tbsp cold-pressed coconut oil or ghee
4 plums, stoned and sliced
1 tbsp maple syrup

To make the porridge, soak the amaranth seeds in cold water for at least 30 minutes or up to 8 hours, then rinse and drain. Place the amaranth, salt and measured water in a heavy-based saucepan. Cover with a lid. Bring to a boil and immediately reduce the heat and cook very gently for about 20 minutes or until creamy.

Meanwhile, to make the caramelized plums, heat the coconut oil in a frying pan over a medium heat. Add the plums and maple syrup and sauté for a couple of minutes.

The plums should be tender and have a sweet scent of fruity caramel.

Remove the amaranth porridge from the heat and let it sit for about 5 minutes. When the porridge has set a bit, stir in the almond milk until you reach the creaminess you desire. Use the leftover almond milk for serving. Serve in bowls and top with the warm maple plums, coconut flakes, a splash of almond milk and a sprinkling of cinnamon. It will keep in the fridge for a few days.

45 BREAKFASTS

# Mexican Breakfast Salad

I'd say we are a part-sweet, part-savoury kind of family – at least when it comes to breakfast. As much as we love our smoothies, porridges and granola, a breakfast wouldn't feel complete without some eggs and greens. If you ask us, Mexicans are the champions of savoury breakfasts. We have had so many great ones in Mexico but also one very scary experience (at least if you are a sensitive vegetarian). At one of our favourite breakfast spots, we ordered large bowls of guacamole, refried black beans and pico de gallo, served with soft-boiled eggs and corn tortillas. It was heaven, until the third day when David found a chunk of bacon in his beans. 'I thought I ordered a vegetarian option?' he asked the chef. 'Yes, yes, this is vegetarian.' 'But what is this, then?' 'Don't worry about that. The beans are just cooked in bacon, it adds flavour. Everybody does that in Mexico.' And those were the last beans David had on our trip. Our version of a warm Mexican breakfast salad has a lovely balance between sweet mango, savoury beans, creamy avocado, sunny eggs, herbs and a fierce kick from the jalapeños. And it is guaranteed bacon-free. — *Luise*

1 tbsp cold-pressed olive or coconut oil,
   ghee or butter
¼ red onion, finely chopped
100 g (3 ½ oz /½ cup) dried black beans,
   soaked and cooked (or a 400 g (14 oz)
   can, drained)
a pinch of chilli powder
a pinch of ground cumin
a pinch of sea salt

1 avocado, halved, stoned, peeled and sliced
1 mango, peeled, and sliced, discarding the stone
juice of ½ lime
5 sprigs of coriander (cilantro), leaves picked
2 eggs
2 tbsp pickled jalapeños, drained

Heat the oil in a frying pan, add the onion, beans, chilli, cumin and salt and stirfry over a medium-low heat for a few minutes. Place in a bowl with the remaining ingredients except the eggs and jalapeños and toss to combine. Divide between 2 serving bowls.

Heat a drizzle of oil in a frying pan over a medium-low heat and fry the egg until set but with a soft yolk. Serve the bean salad straight away, topped with the fried egg and a few jalapeño slices.

49         BREAKFASTS

# Vegan Nut & Seed Bread

I am Danish, so Copenhagen is naturally the destination our family travels to most often. Every time we go back home, we are invited to a smørrebrød gathering at my grandparents' house. They fill their table with different jams, spreads, pickled fish, vegetables and egg salads that we all use to top our rye bread. As the Paleo Diet has become trendy in Denmark, a nut, seed and egg bread has lately started to replace the rye bread on many smørrebrød tables. Even if my grandparents prefer the traditional version and I will never give it up myself, I think the nut bread is brilliant. We have tweaked the original recipe to make it completely vegan.

You can use any seeds or nuts for this recipe, or make it nut-free and add just seeds (made up to the relevant quantity). Remember that the psyllium husks powder is essential for this recipe as an egg substitute. If you can't find it in health food stores, you can order it online – it's not expensive. To use eggs instead, see the tip at the end of the recipe. The bread is also really delicious with added grated vegetables such as carrots, courgettes (zucchini), beetroot (red beets) or apples. — *Luise*

2 tbsp psyllium husks powder
350 ml (12 fl oz/1⅓ cups) water
100 g (3½ oz/⅔ cup) almonds
100 g (3½ oz/⅔ cup) hazelnuts (filberts)
100 g (3½ oz/⅔ cup) sesame seeds
100 g (3½ oz/⅔ cup) sunflower seeds
100 g (3½ oz/⅔ cup) flax seeds

100 g (3½ oz/⅔ cup) pumpkin seeds
1 tsp fine sea salt
3 tbsp melted cold pressed coconut oil or
    olive oil, plus extra for greasing
a handful raisins or chopped dark chocolate
    (optional but delicious)

Preheat the oven to 180°C (350°F/Gas 4). Mix the psyllium husks powder and water very well together in a bowl and set aside for 5 minutes until it forms a thick gel.

Meanwhile, place all the nuts and seeds in a bowl, add the salt, oil and raisins or chocolate, if using, and stir. Add the psyllium gel and give it a good stir with your hands – it is important to combine it well or you will end up with gel-like lumps in your bread. Set aside for 1 hour (this step is optional but the end result will be better). Pour into a greased loaf pan (30 x 10 cm 12 x 4 in) and bake for 60–70 minutes. Alternatively, spoon the batter into a greased 12-cup muffin pan and bake for 45–50 minutes. Remove from the oven and leave to cool completely (we know it is difficult, but it is very important) before slicing. Store wrapped in a clean tea towel in the fridge for up to a week, or put in the freezer – it freezes well.

Tip: Eggs are used in the original Paleo recipe and for a non-vegan version you can replace the psyllium husk powder and water with five eggs. Simply mix into the bread, tip into the tins and bake – there is no need to set aside for an hour.

# Rye & Chocolate Croissants

During the six months I lived in Rome, I took every measure to become 'un vero Italiano' – a true Italian. It wasn't always an easy task – having to wear sunglasses on dark buses, leaving an extra button open on my shirts and learning how to speak with my hands. But it had its bright moments, and breakfast was one of those. Cappuccino and cornetto (the Italian word for croissant) seemed to be part of everyone's morning routine, so they became part of mine too. I often ordered cornetto integrale, which is supposed to be a healthier wholemeal one but at best had only about one per cent of whole grains in it. My version has a much higher ratio. Spelt flour and rye flour add nuttiness and more character to the croissants. They are a little trickier to master, as their gluten content is lower so the dough is less elastic. Try to knead it as little as possible.

What I love about this method is that you prepare the croissants the night before, so all you have to do in the morning is put them in the oven. Start around dinner time if you want to make it to bed before midnight. You can also shape the trimmed-off edges into a bun and bake immediately at 200°C (400°F/ gas 6) for 15 minutes. It's a nice treat for the persistent night-baker. — David

80 g (3 oz/⅔ cup) rye flour, plus extra for
    dusting
185 g (6½ oz/1½ cups) spelt flour
1 tbsp cold-pressed olive oil
175 ml (6 fl oz/¾ cup) GMO-free soya milk
    or milk of choice
1 tbsp maple syrup
2 tsp active dry yeast

½ tsp salt
125 g (4 oz/½ cup) cold butter
4 tbsp homemade Cacao & Hazelnut Spread
    (page 239) or 50 g (2 oz) dark chocolate,
    finely chopped
1 egg, beaten, for brushing

Sift the flours together and set aside. Heat the oil with the milk and maple syrup to lukewarm in a small saucepan. Place the dry yeast and salt in a large bowl and pour the milk over. Add about a quarter of the flour mixture, stir and leave to rest for 10 minutes until bubbles appear. Gradually add the rest of the flour and quickly work it into a non-sticky dough – just a minute or two should be enough. The dough will feel quite firm at this point. Cover the bowl and leave to rest for an hour at room temperature. Turn the dough out on to a floured work surface. Flatten it out, sprinkle a little extra flour on top, fold it together into a tight square then wrap in plastic wrap and chill for 30 minutes.

Remove the dough from the fridge, place on a lightly floured surface and roll it into a rectangle, about 30 x 20 cm (12 x 8 in). Use a cheese cutter, mandolin or sharp knife to cut the butter into thin flakes and spread them in a single layer to cover two-thirds of the dough, leaving a 10 x 20 cm (4 x 8 in) flap uncovered. (Alternatively, you can put the butter between 2 layers of baking parchment and roll it into a 20 cm (8 in) square with a rolling pin and lay it on the dough.) Fold the empty third of the dough over the butter and then take the last third and fold it over the top of the other 2 flaps (like a business letter). Rotate the dough through 90° and roll it out to a similar-sized rectangle again. Fold it up in thirds again then wrap in plastic wrap and chill for 1 hour. Roll and fold the dough again, rewrap and chill for a further hour.

Unwrap the dough and roll it out on a lightly floured surface to a 30 x 20 cm (12 x 8 in) rectangle once more. Trim off the edges with a sharp knife and cut the dough into 4 equal-sized rectangles, then cut each rectangle diagonally, making 8 triangles.

Take 1 triangle. Stretch the corner of the shortest edge, to make the edges more even. Put a heaped teaspoon of Cacao & Hazelnut Spread or dark chocolate in the middle of the triangle, towards the base. Start at the base and with a light touch, roll the croissant up toward the thinnest point. Place it on a baking sheet lined with baking parchment. Shape the rest of the croissants and place well apart on the sheet. Cover with oiled plastic wrap and put in the fridge overnight.

In the morning, remove the croissants from the fridge, unwrap, cover with a clean tea towel (dishcloth) and let them prove for about 1 hour. Meanwhile, preheat the oven to 200°C (400°F/Gas 6). Brush each croissant with beaten egg to glaze. Bake for 20–25 minutes, until deep golden and with a bubbly flaky crust.

Tip: You can of course also bake them without filling or try a savoury filling. Pesto is great. Cheese and mustard is another classic. The spelt flour can be replaced with normal all-purpose flour for an even flakier (but less wholesome) croissant.

# Pumpkin & Almond Waffles

Before our first visit to the USA, we kept pumpkins only as decoration. They are also grown in Europe but have never been as popular or creatively used in recipes as in the States. After spending a few months on the West Coast during pumpkin season, we quickly learned that they can be used in practically any kind of recipe – sweet or savoury. On our trip we made sure to try pumpkin pie, cheesecake and muffins, pumpkin soup and salad, pumpkin pancakes and even pumpkin spice coffee. But of all the sweet combinations, we grew most fond of the spiced pumpkin waffles that we tried in a diner just south of Big Sur, California. They were served with a slab of maple butter and after our third plate we were in a food coma for the rest of the day.

We created these with a similar mixture of spices but slightly lighter, using almond flour and buttermilk. They are still quite rich, so two waffles are usually enough for one person. If pumpkins are out of season, you can use two cups mashed ripe banana instead of the pumpkin purée.

*1 small pumpkin or butternut squash, about 700g (1lb 10 oz) or 500 g (1lb 2 oz/2 cups) unsweetened pumpkin purée*
*6 eggs*
*250 ml (8½ fl oz/1 cup) cultured buttermilk*
*120 ml (4 fl oz/½ cup) water*
*210 g (7½ oz/generous 2 cups) almond flour*
*60 g (2 oz/½ cup) buckwheat flour*
*2 tbsp maple syrup or clear honey (preferably unheated), plus extra to serve*

*1½ tsp baking powder*
*1 tsp ground cinnamon*
*1 tsp ground ginger*
*½ tsp ground cloves*
*½ tsp sea salt*
*a little cold-pressed coconut oil or butter*

*To Serve*
*plain yoghurt*
*Raw Raspberry & Chia Jam (page 232)*

Preheat the oven to 200°C (400°F/Gas 6). Halve the pumpkin with a sharp knife and remove the seeds with a spoon. Place both halves on a baking tray, cut side down, and bake in the oven for 30–40 minutes or until the skin is bubbly and slightly browned and the flesh is soft. Remove the pumpkin from the oven and leave to cool for a couple of minutes. Spoon out the flesh into a bowl. Use a fork (or a food processor) to mash it to a purée.

Whisk the eggs in a large bowl until frothy. Measure 500 g (1lb 2 oz/2 cups) pumpkin purée and add to the bowl together with the remaining ingredients except the coconut

oil or butter. Stir until well combined. Let the batter rest for 15 minutes in the fridge. This is an important step, as the waffles hold together better when baking.

Turn on your waffle iron and wait until it is hot. Brush the grids with a little coconut oil or butter then add about 4 tablespoons of the batter (less or more depending on your waffle iron) and close the lid. The waffle should be ready after about 1½ minutes. Open the lid slowly and use a fork to carefully detach it from the iron. Repeat for the remaining waffles. Serve with a dollop of yoghurt and the Raw Raspberry & Chia Jam and a drizzle of maple syrup.

# Chia & Strawberry Pudding

Regardless of how much we love to travel and eat our way through new countries, it is always a very special feeling to come home to our own kitchen and prepare something that we have longed for. After having been overwhelmed with new flavours, this mild, fruit-topped chia pudding is usually exactly what we crave. It is fresh and light and at the same time very rich, sweet and nourishing. Chia seeds can magically change the consistency of any liquid into a pudding and we often have them for breakfast, snack or dessert. They are a good source of complete protein and have high fibre content, a good ratio of omega three and omega six fatty acids and great antioxidant powers.

*Pudding*
400 ml (14 fl oz/1¾ cups) unsweetened almond
   milk or any milk of your choice
50 g (2 oz/scant ½ cup) chia seeds
½ tsp vanilla extract or ground vanilla
a tiny pinch of sea salt

*Strawberry Sauce*
200 g (7 oz/1½ cups) strawberries (during winter
   we use frozen organic berries)
4 prunes, pitted
a splash of water

*Topping*
1 kiwifruit, cubed
1 apple, cubed
1 avocado, cubed
a sprinkling of cacao nibs
a few mint leaves, chopped

Place the milk, chia seeds, vanilla and salt in a bowl and stir well. Leave in the fridge for an hour or overnight. The seeds will expand and take on a gel-like consistency. Meanwhile, make the strawberry sauce. Place all the ingredients in a small saucepan, bring to the boil, reduce the heat and simmer for 10 minutes. Pour into a bowl, mash with a fork and place in the fridge until chilled and thickened.

Spoon the pudding into 2 large glasses. Top with a couple of spoonfuls of strawberry sauce and cubed kiwi, apple and avocado. Sprinkle with cacao nibs and chopped mint leaves and serve. The chia pudding and the sauce will keep in the fridge for 3–5 days.

   Tip: if you like your chia pudding sweeter, add half a mashed ripe banana to the chia mixture.

# STREET
# FOOD & SNACKS

# Halloumi Veggie Burgers

It's a common misapprehension that you can just stick two fried halloumi slices inside a burger bun, fill it up with some fresh cucumber, tomatoes and lettuce and call it a halloumi burger. I'm the first to admit that it's a quick and delicious treat, but a burger? Nah. Try instead to coarsely grate the halloumi together with carrots, courgettes (zucchini) and some fresh mint and fry it for a couple of minutes in a pan. Then you'll have yourself a proper halloumi burger. We first got the idea for these burgers at a food stall at one of the Sunday markets in London. There they served it almost like we have done here, on a cabbage leaf and with a yoghurt dressing, but you could also just go all the way with classic burger buns. We have fried these in a pan, but you could also put them on a barbecue.

*Burgers*
*1 small courgette (zucchini)*
*1 large carrot*
*200 g (7 oz) halloumi cheese*
*5 sprigs of mint, leaves picked and chopped*

*Tahini Dressing*
*120 ml (4 fl oz/½ cup) plain yoghurt*
*2 tbsp tahini (sesame paste)*
*2 tbsp lime juice*
*1 tsp maple syrup or clear honey (preferably unheated)*
*a pinch of sea salt*

*To Serve*
*large green leaves, like savoy cabbage*
*pea sprouts*
*avocado*
*lettuce*
*sauerkraut (fermented cabbage)*

Grate the courgette, carrot and halloumi cheese on a box grater on the coarsest side. Place in a bowl, add the mint and toss to combine. Form six patties with your hands.

Stir all the tahini dressing ingredients together in a small bowl.

Heat a dry, non-stick frying pan and fry the patties on each side until golden and soft. Serve in a large cabbage leaf with a dollop of tahini dressing, some pea sprouts and sliced avocado and a spoonful of sauerkraut. The patties and the dressing can be stored in the fridge for 3–5 days.

# Crispy Aubergine Bites with Honey & Lime

We first tried *Berenjenas con miel* – deep-fried aubergine bites with honey – in a tapas restaurant in Barcelona. We love the simplicity of the ingredients and the way it's served. Inside the crust, the aubergine (eggplant) is soft as butter and it is flavoured with fresh lime and a drizzle of sweet honey. It is just a wonderful combination – fresh, sweet and savoury. Here we oven-bake the aubergine wedges instead of frying them. They only need a light drizzle with oil to become crisp on the outside and deliciously soft inside.

1 aubergine (eggplant)
500 ml (17 fl oz/2¼ cups) milk of your choice
150 g (5½ oz/1 cup) polenta (GMO-free organic
  fine cornmeal)
2 tsp coarse sea salt, plus extra for serving
a little cold-pressed olive oil

**To Serve**
finely grated zest of 2 limes
2 tbsp clear honey (preferably unheated)

Cut the aubergine into small wedges, around 7.5 cm (3 in) long. Place them in a large bowl and cover them with the milk. Leave to soak for about an hour to draw out the bitterness. Set the oven to 220°C (425°F/Gas 7) and line a baking sheet with baking parchment.

Mix the polenta with the sea salt in a shallow bowl. Remove the aubergine from the milk and coat the wedges in polenta. Turn a couple of times to make sure they are evenly coated, then place them on the prepared baking sheet. Drizzle lightly with olive oil and bake for about 12 minutes or until lightly golden and crispy and soft on the inside. Serve topped with some extra sea salt, lime zest and honey drizzled on top.

# Lentil & Strawberry Tacos

Taco traditionalists beware – you might find the following recipe intimidating. Our version of tacos is definitely a far cry from the original. As much as we love all the vegetable tacos and cheese enchiladas we have tried at restaurants in Mexico and food trucks in southern California, they simply felt too greasy for this book. But that said, we couldn't turn our backs on the idea of wrapping up vegetables in a warm corn tortilla and eating it up straight away, so here we present a fresh and beautiful vegan alternative with mashed avocado, a lentil, cabbage and strawberry filling and our own Pico de Gallo Spread (page 234).

*200 g (7 oz/1 cup) beluga lentils*
*450 ml (15 fl oz/2 cups) water*
*sea salt and freshly ground pepper*
*½ small cabbage, finely shredded*
*1 handful fresh strawberries, thinly sliced*
*1 tbsp cold-pressed olive oil*
*2 tbsp hemp seeds (optional)*
*2 avocados, halved and stoned*
*a squeeze of lime or lemon juice*
*8 GMO-free corn tortillas*

*To Serve*
*Pico de Gallo Spread (page 234)*
*1 handful sprouts or micro greens, for topping*

Rinse and drain the lentils. Place in a saucepan and add the water and a pinch of sea salt. Cover with a lid and bring to the boil. Lower the heat immediately and simmer gently for about 20 minutes or until tender. Drain any excess water and set aside to cool.

Meanwhile, place the cabbage and strawberries in a bowl, drizzle with olive oil and season with salt and pepper. Add the hemp seeds, if using, and gently toss to combine, using your hands.

Scoop out the avocado flesh into a bowl, add a squeeze of lime or lemon juice (especially if not using immediately) and mash with a fork. Warm the tortillas. To serve, take a tortilla, add some mashed avocado, a spoonful of Pico de Gallo Spread and a couple of spoonfuls of lentil filling and top with sprouts or micro greens. Fold up the edges to hold the taco in your hands and enjoy!

# Lemongrass & Coconut Summer Rolls

Summer rolls, or fresh spring rolls as they are also known, were a family favourite long before we visited Vietnam. There simply is no fresher food, with crunchy lettuce leaves, fresh herbs and all kind of good stuff all rolled in thin rice paper and dipped in salty sauces. What we learned in Vietnam was to marinade tofu with lemongrass and to add grated coconut to the rolls both for the flavour and texture.

*200 g (7 oz) organic, GMO-free firm tofu*
*2 lemongrass stalks, crushed and very finely chopped*
*juice of 1 lime*
*1 tsp maple syrup*
*2 tsp organic, GMO-free soy sauce*

### Dipping Sauce
*25 g (1 oz/⅓ cup) raw peanuts*
*2 tbsp rice vinegar*
*2 tbsp organic, GMO-free soy sauce*
*2 tbsp cold water*
*1 tbsp maple syrup*

### To Serve
*1 packet of rice paper*
*1 round (butterhead) lettuce, rinsed and leaves separated*
*a large handful mint, leaves picked*
*a large handful coriander (cilantro), leaves picked*
*½ cucumber, cut into sticks*
*1 mango, peeled, flesh cut into sticks, discarding stone*
*30 g (1 oz/½ cup) unsweetened coconut flakes (chips)*
*30 g (1 oz/½ cup) sprouts (mung bean, broccoli, pea, alfalfa)*

Pat the tofu dry with kitchen paper. Cut it into thick sticks and place on a large, deep plate. Stir together the rest of the ingredients and pour over the tofu. Leave to marinate for at least 30 minutes, turning over once.

To make the dipping sauce, lightly toast the peanuts in a frying pan over a medium-low heat. Tip out of the pan immediately, cool slightly then finely chop. Stir the peanuts together with all the remaining sauce ingredients in a small bowl and set aside.

Put all the different filling ingredients in separate bowls and arrange next to a chopping board along with a bowl of warm water. To serve, dip a sheet of rice paper into the bowl of warm water for a few seconds, until softened. Lay it on the chopping board. Layer a lettuce leaf with some mint and coriander leaves, cucumber and mango sticks, a few coconut flakes, sprouts and a marinated tofu stick. Fold the top over the filling, tuck the filling in, fold in the sides and then roll up. Place on a serving platter. Repeat with the remaining rolls.

Serve with the dipping sauce.

# Grilled Lemon & Herb Corn Cobs

Well-grilled corn-on-the-cob should be so juicy that it splatters over your teeth on the first bite. We have tried it in almost every part of the world we have been to and have picked up a few tricks on how best to prepare it. First, and most importantly, make sure to choose corn cobs that look tight and fresh, with large, round, creamy-yellow corn kernels (avoid if deep gold as the sugar will be turning to starch so they will be less sweet). Second, soak them in their husks before grilling to allow them to be simultaneously slightly steamed.

The seasoning can differ quite a bit between the continents, from the cheese, mayo and coriander (cilantro)-topped corn in Mexico to the sweet chilli-spiced corn in Asia. Our favourite way of seasoning it is simply slathered with a homemade herb butter and a good grinding of black pepper.

*4 GMO-free corn cobs with husks*

*Herb Butter*
*1 large handful mixed fresh herbs (basil,
    rosemary, chives, sage, thyme, parsley etc.)*
*125 g (4 oz/½ cup) butter, at room
    temperature*
*finely grated zest of 1 lemon*
*sea salt and ground black pepper*

Chop the herbs very finely. Combine all the herb butter ingredients with a little salt and plenty of black pepper in a small bowl. Stir to mix well. Transfer the butter to a sheet of baking parchment and use it to roll the butter into a log. Twist the ends to seal. Chill until the butter is firm or, if you are short of time, transfer to the freezer for about 10 minutes.

Soak the corn cobs in their husks in cold water for 15 minutes and then drain well by shaking them upside down. This soaking gives extra moisture to the corn cobs and they won't be dry after grilling. Prepare a hot barbecue, or place a griddle pan over a high heat. Arrange the corn cobs with husks directly on the barbecue rack or place in the pan and cook, turning as needed, for 15–20 minutes, until nicely marked on all sides without being burned. Remove the husks and serve with thick slices of the herb butter to smear all over the kernels.

# Tempeh & Papaya Satay Skewers

Many years ago, Luise and I spent a couple of weeks backpacking and eating our way around Bali, Indonesia. We tried crispy and thin cassava chips, many peanut butter and fragrant rice dishes, the horrifically odorous durian fruit and a wide array of vegetable skewers (along with a really nasty microwave pizza that will probably never leave our memory).

Tempeh is a fermented soya bean cake that is common all around Indonesia, and now also around the world. High in protein, it contains healthy bacteria from the fermentation and is a good alternative to meat for vegetarians. It's available fresh or frozen from some health food stores or online. We marinate the tempeh in a sweet soy sauce and spear it on skewers together with papaya. When papaya isn't completely fresh and ripe it often lacks flavour, but when grilled it releases its juice and becomes all sweet and yummy. — *David*

*Peanut & Coconut Sauce*
4 tbsp peanut or almond butter
120 ml (4 fl oz/½ cup) full-fat coconut milk
juice of 1 lime
½ tsp ground coriander
½ tsp ground cumin

*Tempeh Skewers*
225 g (8 oz) GMO-free fresh or thawed
  frozen tempeh
2 tbsp GMO-free soy sauce
2 tbsp maple syrup
1 tsp grated fresh ginger
½ small papaya (persimmon, pineapple
  or peach would also be good)

*To Serve*
a few whole lettuce leaves
a handful mint, leaves picked
a handful coriander (cilantro), leaves
  picked and roughly chopped
lime wedges

First make the sauce. Place all the ingredients in a small saucepan and cook over a low heat, stirring until everything is combined. Tip into a small bowl, leave to cool then chill until ready to serve.

Cut the tempeh into thick slices. Stir together the soy sauce, maple syrup and grated ginger in a bowl. Place the tempeh in the marinade, turn to coat a couple of times and leave to marinate for about 10 minutes.

Peel the papaya, remove the seeds and cut into slices the same size as the tempeh. Thread the papaya and marinated

tempeh onto skewers (soaked first, if bamboo or wooden), either alternately on the same skewers or on separate ones.

Heat a non-stick frying pan and fry the skewers on each side for a few minutes, or cook on a hot barbecue for 3–5 minutes, turning as needed, until nicely marked on all sides without being burned.

Brush the skewers with the remaining marinade while they are being grilled. Serve with the chilled sauce, a few lettuce leaves, fresh mint, coriander and some lime wedges to squeeze over.

# Rosemary Baked Chestnuts

My stepdad is Italian so I got to spend a lot of summers and Christmases around Naples as a kid. I have so many food-related memories from those years. Most of them involved Nonna's (my grandmother's) traditional Italian cooking, but another memory that always comes to mind around December is wandering the Neapolitan streets with my family and buying warm roasted chestnuts from the street vendors. It was many years ago, but this is how I remember having them: wrapped in paper with fresh rosemary, butter, salt and a zing of fresh lemon zest. — *Luise*

*500 g (1 lb 2 oz) fresh unshelled chestnuts*
*10 small knobs of butter*
*4 sprigs of rosemary, torn into smaller stems*
*1 tbsp coarse sea salt*
*finely grated zest of 1 lemon*

Preheat the oven to 180°C (350°F/Gas 4).

Use a sharp knife to carefully cut a cross on the round side of each chestnut. Place them all in a baking dish and dot with the butter, rosemary, salt and lemon zest. Roast in the oven for 35 minutes or until golden and the shells have opened slightly. They are best eaten while still warm, but they are also a great addition to salads. Simply peel off the outer and inner skins (they'll come away together for the most part) and enjoy.

# Masala Dosa

'How is this?' Luise wobbles her head from side to side, trying to get the Indian head shake right. It looks pretty convincing, or should I say confusing. It can mean 'yes', but it can also mean 'okay, I hear you', or even 'no'. We are sitting on the plane on the way back from Trivandrum in southern India and are talking about all the things that we will miss. 'I will definitely miss that it's all right to eat with my hands,' I admit. 'Ha! That's why you feel so at home there.' Luise is right. I have always preferred eating with my hands instead of a fork and in India I can do so freely without anyone thinking I am weird. 'I am going to miss the breakfast dosa,' Luise sighs. We have had the spicy lentil pancakes filled with peas and potatoes for both breakfast and quick street food. We asked about the method and it involves a few rather complicated steps of soaking rice and lentils and then mixing them into a batter that you leave to ferment – not exactly a quick breakfast in our home. For this book, we have created a quicker version using chickpea and brown rice flour — *David*

*Sweet Potato Filling*
ghee or cold-pressed coconut oil, for frying,
 plus extra for the dosa
1 onion, finely chopped
1 tsp garam masala spice blend
¼ tsp ground ginger
¼ tsp ground turmeric
¼ tsp chilli powder
2 sweet potatoes, boiled, peeled and cubed
150g (5 oz/1 cup) fresh shelled or thawed
 frozen peas
1 small handful coriander (cilantro)

*Indian Mint & Coconut Raita*
6 tbsp plain yoghurt (or a vegan alternative)
20 g (¾ oz/1 cup) mint, finely chopped
4 tbsp unsweetened desiccated (shredded) coconut

*Chickpea Dosa*
125 g (4 oz/1 cup) chickpea flour
40 g (1½ oz/¼ cup) brown rice flour
1 tsp sea salt
1 tbsp nigella seeds (optional)
250 ml (8½ fl oz/1 cup) water

*To Serve*
Mango & Raisin Chutney (page 243)
½ tsp ghee or coconut oil

Heat a knob of ghee or coconut oil in a frying pan over a medium heat and add the onion and all the spices. Stir frequently and cook until fragrant. Add the cooked sweet potatoes and peas and cook until hot through, stirring. Mash with the back of a wooden spoon and sprinkle with the coriander. Set aside while preparing the raita and the dosa.

To make the raita, combine all the ingredients in a small serving bowl. Add more yoghurt if you prefer a looser consistency. Chill until ready to serve. It will keep in the fridge for a couple of days.

To make the dosa, mix the flours in a bowl with the salt and nigella seeds, if using. Gradually whisk in the water to make quite a thick batter.

Add the ghee or coconut oil to a frying pan over a medium-high heat. Add about a quarter of the batter to the pan and immediately use a spoon to smooth it out into a circle. Turn when golden and brown the other side. Slide out of the pan and keep warm while making the remaining dosa. Add a few tablespoons of filling to each dosa and fold in a loose roll, ready to serve with the raita and chutney.

# SALADS & SIDES

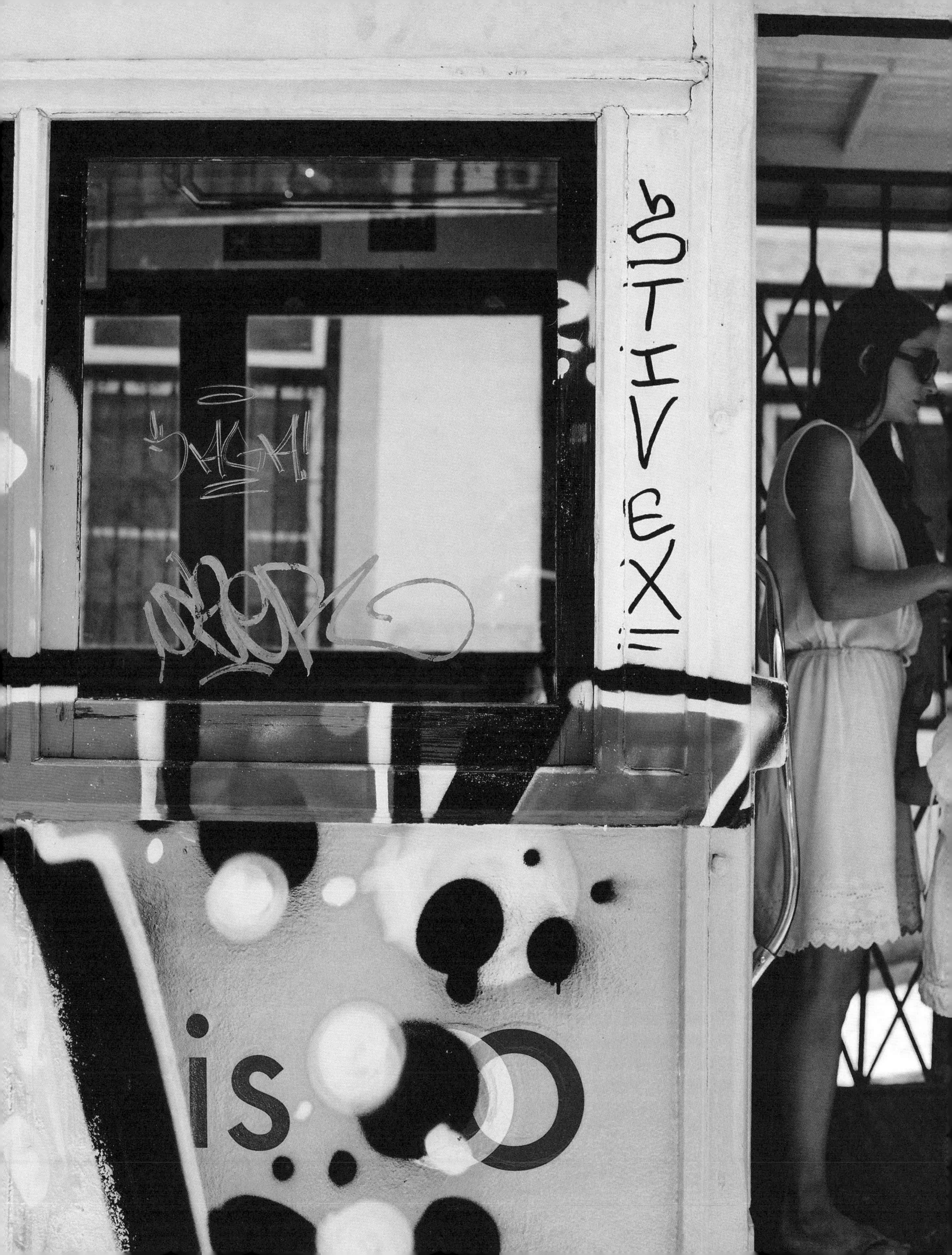
STIVEX
is

# August Market Cherry Salad

David's family has an apartment in Barcelona, so it has become somewhat of a third home to us. Being there inevitably means eating lots of tapas, olive oil-drenched vegetables and croquettes. But we also love to head down to one of the vegetable markets for a bag of fresh produce and prepare a big salad at home. In August the cherries are dark red and along with so many other fruit and vegetables they are bursting with flavour, so a trip to the market during that period is like going to the sweet shop. We have used both the celery stalks and the top leaves in this salad recipe, as they have a pleasant bite that is hard to find in any other greens. Combined with the creamy avocado and goats' cheese and sweet cherries, they make a salad that's packed with colour, taste and texture. — *Luise*

*1 small celery head sliced, including the leaves*
*2 avocados, stoned, peeled and sliced*
*2 handfuls cherry tomatoes, halved*
*2 large handfuls cherries, halved and stoned*
*1 small bunch flat-leaf parsley, leaves picked*
*    and finely chopped*
*juice of ½ lemon or more to taste*
*1 tbsp cold-pressed olive oil*
*a pinch of coarse sea salt and freshly*
*    ground black pepper*
*200 g (7 oz) soft goats' cheese, crumbled*

Rinse and prepare all the vegetables, fruit and herbs and place in a large serving bowl. Mix to combine. Add the lemon juice, olive oil, salt and pepper and toss to mix well. Scatter with the crumbled cheese and serve. The salad will keep in the fridge for a couple of days.

# Sicilian Caponata

One of the first journeys that Luise and I made together was a road trip in Sicily. We drove around the island with neither a map nor any accommodation booked in advance. I suppose it was a good way to test our fresh relationship. We had a blast. Sometimes we ended up in the most amazing places, such as a hotel from the 1920s, perched on the clifftop in Taormina, with a stunning view and freshly squeezed juice from their own orange grove. Other times ... well, they were not as mind-blowing. We even spent one night sleeping in the car, to save our budget after a few too many extravagant restaurant bills. Another trick to keep our expenses to a minimum was to restrict our lunches to a single serving of caponata. This vegetable-packed dish is normally served as a side in Italy, but when combined with some bread it is enough to keep a young couple happy until dinner. Nowadays we still make this as a main course, together with some wholegrain pasta or thinly shaved zucchini noodles, but it can also be served as a side to most dishes. — *David*

*2 tbsp cold-pressed olive oil, plus extra*
*    for drizzling*
*1 large aubergine (eggplant), cut into large cubes*
*1 red (bell) pepper, seeded and cut into*
*    large cubes*
*2 tsp dried oregano*
*½ tsp dried chilli flakes*
*2 garlic cloves, sliced*
*1 small onion, finely chopped*
*1 small handful parsley, finely chopped*
*1 small handful mint leaves, finely chopped*
*4 ripe tomatoes, cut into large cubes*
*1 large handful (about 250 g/9 oz/1⅔ cups)*
*    green olives, pitted*
*4 tbsp pickled capers, drained*
*2 tbsp apple cider vinegar*

Heat the oil in a large frying pan. Add aubergine, pepper, oregano and chilli and cook over a medium heat for about 5 minutes, stirring occasionally. When the aubergine and pepper are browned on all sides, add the garlic, onion, most of the parsley and mint (reserving a little for garnish) and cook for another 3 minutes, stirring occasionally. Add a little more oil if needed. Then add the tomatoes, olives, capers and apple cider vinegar and cook for another 20 minutes or until very tender and the aubergine feels very soft.

Serve garnished with the reserved chopped fresh herbs, a drizzle of olive oil. Eat with a piece of wholegrain sourdough bread, if you wish. This can be stored in the fridge for 3–5 days.

# Quinoa, Almond & Mint Salad

Moroccan couscous salads have the most wonderful mix of flavours, and sweet raisins, crunchy salted almonds and fresh herbs are an irresistible combination. We make our version gluten-free by using white protein-rich quinoa which we cook together with cinnamon. We marinate the courgette (zucchini) and aubergine (eggplant) ourselves, but for a quicker version you can get them ready-marinated in glass jars from most food stores.

*1 courgette (zucchini)*
*1 aubergine (eggplant)*
*2 tbsp cold-pressed olive oil, plus extra*
*    for grilling*
*1 garlic clove, crushed*
*sea salt*
*300 g (10½ oz/1½ cups) quinoa*
*750 ml (25 fl oz/3 cups) water*
*1 tsp ground cinnamon*
*juice of ½ lemon,*
*a handful mint leaves*
*1 handful coriander (cilantro) leaves*
*2 avocados, cut into small dice*
*3 tbsp brown or golden raisins*
*1 pomegranate, seeds scooped out and separated*
*100 g (3½ oz/ scant 1 cup) toasted,*
*    salted almonds*

To marinate the vegetables, preheat the oven to 200°C (400°F/ Gas 6). Slice the aubergine and courgette into thin rounds. Place on a grill rack in a baking tin and use a pastry brush to brush them lightly with oil on both sides. Sprinkle with salt and roast in the oven until soft and slightly burned on the edges, about 15 minutes – keep an eye on them, as they burn easily. Remove the vegetables from the oven and place in a bowl. Add the olive oil and garlic and set aside.

Rinse the quinoa well in water and drain. Place in a saucepan and add the measured water, ground cinnamon and ½ teaspoon salt. Bring to the boil, reduce the heat immediately. Cover and simmer gently for 15–20 minutes.

To assemble the salad, place the cooked quinoa in a large serving bowl and leave to cool slightly. Add the lemon juice, herbs, roasted vegetables, avocado and raisins and toss until everything is well combined.

Garnish with the pomegranate seeds and almonds. Serve or store in the fridge in an airtight container for 3–5 days.

# Brussels Sprout & Cranberry Holiday Salad

The problem with Brussels sprouts and kale is that they are often overcooked and turned into limp, soggy messes. We prefer our greens vigorously sturdy, with a texture that offers a bit of a chew. This American-inspired salad is just that. It has nuts for extra crunch, oranges for a fruity aroma and a classic mustard and honey dressing that is simultaneously fierce and sweet. It's good on any occasion but perfect during the winter holiday season.

*200 g (7 oz/1 cup) beluga lentils*
  *or lentils of your choice*
*450 ml (15 fl oz/2 cups) water*
*500 g (1 lb 2 oz) Brussels sprouts*
*250 g (9 oz) kale (any variety)*
*100 g (3½ oz/1 cup) raw pecan nuts*
*2 oranges*
*75 g (2½ oz/½ cup) cup fresh or*
  *thawed frozen cranberries*

***Mustard Dressing***
*2 tbsp made English mustard*
  *(gluten-free if intolerant)*
*2 tbsp clear honey (preferably unheated)*
*6 tbsp cold-pressed olive oil*
*juice of 1 small lemon*
*a pinch of coarse sea salt*

Rinse and drain the lentils. Place in a saucepan and add the measured water. Cover with a lid and bring to the boil, then reduce the heat and cook gently for about 20 minutes or until tender and the water has been absorbed. Set aside to cool. Meanwhile, bring a large pot of water to the boil.

Trim and shred the Brussels sprouts very finely with a sharp knife, or use a food processor. Shred the kale very finely, discarding any thick central stalks. Place the shredded Brussels sprouts in the boiling water and blanch them for no more than a minute. Drain through a colander and rinse immediately in cold water. Pat dry.

Toast the nuts in a dry frying pan over a medium heat until browned and crispy, taking care not to burn them. Peel the oranges and cut into small wedges.

Prepare the dressing by whisking all ingredients in a small bowl, then set aside.

Place the shredded kale in a large bowl, add half of the dressing and use your hands to massage the kale for a couple of minutes or until it becomes soft. Now add the drained Brussels sprouts and toss to combine. Add the nuts, oranges and cranberries to the greens and toss with your hands to mix.

Serve straight away or leave for an hour or so for the flavours to develop.

# Farro Salad

We often buy this kind of salad in Italian delis, along with large containers of marinated artichokes, olives and peppers, a few different versions of fresh ricotta, taleggio and mozzarella cheeses and some freshly baked *pane integrale*. It's simple Mediterranean no-fuss food that tastes amazing. It is also great to bring on picnics, as it can be brutally handled without turning ugly and can be served both cold and warm. The basic idea of this salad is to combine any sort of grain berries with finely chopped, oven-baked vegetables and a generous drizzle of olive oil. Roasted root vegetables could be good as a variation, too. Vegans will need to leave out the cheese at the end.

*225g (8 oz/generous 1 cup) farro (wheat berries),*
  *oat grains or pearl barley or buckwheat*
*1 green courgette (zucchini)*
*1 yellow (bell) pepper, halved and seeded*
*1 fennel bulb, any green fronds reserved*
*15 ripe small tomatoes*
*2 garlic cloves, crushed*
*a little cold-pressed olive oil*

*sea salt and freshly ground pepper*
*juice of 1 lemon*
*a handful basil, finely chopped*
*a handful mint, finely chopped*
*150 g (5 oz/scant 1 cup) olives, pitted*
*25 g (1 oz/¼ cup) shelled raw pistachios,*
  *coarsely chopped*
*some fresh Parmesan or Pecorino cheese,*
  *shaved (optional)*

Place the farro in a bowl, cover with twice as much water and soak for at least 1 hour (maximum 12 hours). Meanwhile, preheat the oven to 200°C (400°F/Gas 6). Chop the courgette, pepper, fennel, and tomatoes into small cubes. Place on a baking tray, add the garlic and drizzle with olive oil. Sprinkle with salt and pepper and give the mixture a good toss with your hands. Roast in the oven for 30 minutes until soft with slightly crispy edges. Carefully stir every now and then.

Drain the farro, place in a saucepan and add twice as much fresh water. Bring to the boil, reduce the heat and simmer for 15–20 minutes until tender. Add ½ teaspoon sea salt towards the end of the cooking time. Remove from the heat and drain any excess water.

Place the cooked farro in a mixing bowl together with the lemon juice and a drizzle of olive oil. Add the roasted vegetables, finely chopped herbs, olives and pistachios and toss to mix. Shave a few large slices of Parmesan cheese on top before serving, if using. The salad can be stored in an airtight container in the fridge for 3–5 days.

Tip: Some people with gluten intolerance can eat oat grains. They don't contain gluten but avenin, a similar protein. However oats are often contaminated with gluten from wheat, barley or rye during processing so you need to check the label if you need them to be totally gluten-free.

For another safe gluten-free alternative use whole buckwheat.

# A Mix of Six Moroccan Salads

If you order a Moroccan salad in a restaurant, you can never be quite sure what you'll get. Sometimes it is a simple tomato and red onion salad, but most of the time it is something that we would normally call a spread of pickled vegetables. They can come in a variety of different versions; we have included six here. We were taught how to make these by a Moroccan chef at the beautiful restaurant Le Jardine in Marrakech. At home we usually settle for one or two of them, but Moroccans fill the table with an array of colourful salads and eat them with warm pitta bread. The salads are all wonderful in their own right; some are deliciously sweet, some are fiercely intense and others are simple and fresh. These could be great to serve for larger gatherings, together with some dark bread and an assortment of cheeses.

# Aubergine Zaalouk

*2 aubergines (eggplant)*
*2 garlic cloves*
*1–2 tbsp cold-pressed olive or coconut oil*
*1 tbsp ground cumin*
*1 tsp ground paprika*
*½ tsp sea salt*
*120 ml (4 fl oz/½ cup) boiling water*
*2 tbsp tomato purée (paste)*
*5 mm (¼ in) slice lemon, finely chopped*
*1 handful mixed coriander (cilantro)*
  *and parsley leaves*

Chop the aubergines into bite-sized pieces and mash the garlic with the back of a knife. Heat the oil in a large frying pan, then add the garlic and chopped aubergine. When the aubergine is just beginning to stick to the frying pan, stir and add the cumin, paprika and salt.

Add the boiling water and tomato purée and stir to combine. Now add the chopped lemon and fresh herbs, cover with a lid and cook gently for about 45 minutes or until the aubergine is completely soft. Add more water if needed during cooking to prevent drying out. Taste and adjust the flavours. Serve immediately or store in an airtight glass jar in the fridge for up to 5 days.

# Lemony Pepper & Tomato Salad

4 red (bell) peppers
6 tomatoes
4 garlic cloves
½ tsp sea salt
2 tbsp lemon juice

Preheat the oven to 200°C (400°F/Gas 6). Place the peppers in an ovenproof dish and roast in the oven for about 30 minutes, turning occasionally, until the skin is bubbling and blackened. Remove from the oven and leave to cool slightly while preparing the rest of the ingredients.

Chop the tomatoes and mash the garlic with the back of a knife. Discard the skin, stalk and seeds from the roasted peppers, then coarsely chop and set aside. Heat the oil in a frying pan over a medium heat and add the garlic and tomatoes. Cook for about 5 minutes until soft and juicy. Add the roasted peppers and salt and cook for a further 5 minutes. Add the lemon juice, taste and add more salt if necessary. Serve or store in an airtight glass jar in the fridge for up to 5 days.

# Marinated Carrots

5 large carrots, about 500 g (1lb 2 oz)
½ tsp ground cumin
juice of ½ lemon
a splash of cold-pressed olive oil

Peel the carrots and cut into bite-sized pieces. Place in a saucepan and cover with water. Bring to the boil, reduce the heat and simmer for 8–10 minutes or until tender. Remove from the heat and drain the excess water. Place in a serving bowl and leave to cool.

Add the cumin, lemon juice and a splash of olive oil. Toss to mix and it is ready to serve. Serve immediately or store in an airtight glass jar in the fridge for 3–5 days.

# Pickled Quince

4 quinces or unripe pears
½ vanilla pod
5 cloves
2 cinnamon sticks
3 tbsp golden or brown raisins
1 tbsp clear honey (preferably unheated)

Raw quinces are very hard, so be careful when peeling and removing the seeds with a sharp knife. Slice them thinly and place in a saucepan. Cover with water and add all spices and the raisins. Cook on a very gentle simmer for 10 minutes or until tender (pears will take a little less time). Turn off the heat, add the honey and stir to dissolve. Serve warm or cold, or store covered with the spiced juice in the fridge for up to 3 days.

Tip: Add 1 teaspoon orange blossom water.

# Cinnamon Flavoured Pumpkin Mash

1 pumpkin or other winter squash,
    such as butternut
a knob of cold-pressed coconut oil
1 tbsp ground cinnamon
1 cinnamon stick

Preheat the oven to 200°C (400°F/Gas 6). Halve the pumpkin, scoop out the seeds and then peel it. Cut the flesh into cubes and place in a mixing bowl. Rub the squares with coconut oil, using your hands, and dust with ground cinnamon. Tip out on a baking sheet covered with baking parchment and spread out evenly. Tuck in the cinnamon stick. Bake in the oven for 20–40 minutes, depending on the oven and the size of the pumpkin cubes. They are done when completely soft, with golden edges. Place in a bowl and crush a little with the back of a spoon. Garnish with the cinnamon stick. Serve immediately or store in an airtight glass jar in the fridge for 3–5 days.

# Marinated Courgettes

1–2 tbsp cold-pressed olive or coconut oil
2 courgettes (zucchini)
1 garlic clove
1 tbsp ground cumin
1 tsp ground paprika
½ tsp sea salt
120 ml (4 fl oz/½ cup) boiling water
2 tbsp tomato purée (paste)
2 tsp apple cider vinegar
1 handful mixed coriander (cilantro)
    and parsley leaves

Divide the courgettes lengthwise and slice each half into bite-sized pieces. Mash the garlic with the back of a knife. Heat the oil in a large frying pan and add the garlic and courgettes. When the courgettes are beginning to stick to the frying pan, stir and add the cumin, paprika and salt. Add the boiling water, tomato purée and vinegar and stir to combine. Cover with a lid and simmer gently for 15–20 minutes or until the courgettes are completely soft. Add more water during cooking if necessary to prevent drying out. Taste and adjust the seasoning if necessary. Serve immediately or store in an airtight glass jar in the fridge for 3–5 days.

TOP: Marinated Courgettes; TOP RIGHT: Lemony Pepper & Tomato Salad; CENTRE LEFT: Marinated Carrots; CENTRE: Pickled Quince; BOTTOM LEFT: Aubergine Zaalouk; BOTTOM: Cinnamon Flavoured Pumpkin Mash

# Upside-Down Beet Tower

Even if this dish has no obvious relation to Mexico, it is inspired by one that we had at a restaurant there. After too many days of tacos, burritos and enchiladas, this fresh salad seemed almost too good to be true. Beetroot (red beets), lettuce, carrots and avocado are shredded, mixed with lime, herbs and olive oil, stuffed into a container, turned out onto a plate and topped with goats' cheese. It's a different way to enjoy a salad and the method can be adapted to any set of ingredients.

5 large lettuce leaves
4 raw beetroot (red beets)
2 carrots
½ cucumber
½ red onion
5 cherry tomatoes
3 avocados
1 handful coriander (cilantro) leaves
   or flat-leaf parsley
2 tbsp cold-pressed olive oil
juice of 1–2 limes (start with the juice
   from 1 lime and adjust to your taste)
sea salt and freshly ground black pepper

*To Serve*
4 or 8 slices goat or sheeps' cheese
   (depending on the size of the cheese)
2 tbsp pine nuts (pine kernels), lightly toasted
1 handful pea sprouts

Coarsely chop the lettuce leaves and place in a large mixing bowl. Peel the beetroot and carrots and grate on a box grater on the coarsest side, or use the grating attachment on a food processor. Slice the cucumber, onion and tomatoes very thinly. Halve, stone, peel and dice the avocados. Chop the herbs. Add all the prepared ingredients to the mixing bowl. Add the olive oil, the juice of 1 lime and salt and pepper. Toss well, using your hands, so everything is coated in oil and lime and has a nice purple colour. Taste and add more lime juice if necessary.

Pack a quarter of the salad mixture tightly into a ramekin dish (custard cup) or dariole mould. Place a serving plate on top of the container and carefully invert, then slowly remove the container. Top the veggie tower with 1 or 2 slices of goats' cheese (if using), toasted pine nuts and pea sprouts. Make 3 more towers in the same way. Enjoy!

# Pomelo, Coconut & Lemongrass Salad

Although I'm a big fan of all kinds of fruit for dessert, I think pomelo is one that is better suited for use in savoury dishes. It's thick and rather dry flesh makes it perfect to coat in a dressing. The flavours in this salad are incredibly fresh and quite sweet, while the coconut and cashews add a nice crunch. If you can't find pomelo you can replace it with grapefruit, but you might want to use a little extra honey to balance the acidity. — *David*

*a handful desiccated (shredded) coconut*
*a handful raw cashew nuts*
*1 pomelo or 2 grapefruit*
*1 stalk of lemongrass, very finely chopped*
*½ red onion, very finely chopped*
*a handful coriander (cilantro) leaves*

*Dressing*
*juice of 2 limes*
*2 tbsp clear honey (preferably unheated)*
  *or maple syrup*
*4 tbsp cold-pressed olive or rapeseed oil*

Toast the coconut and cashew nuts in a dry frying pan over a low heat, stirring occasionally, until golden. Tip out of the pan immediately to prevent over-browning.

Cut off both ends of the pomelo then cut vertical slices into the peel and down the sides. Pull off the slices of peel. Separate the flesh into segments and pull away the membrane that surrounds each slice. Separate the slices into slightly smaller pieces. Place in a large mixing bowl, add the remaining ingredients and toss to mix. Stir together the dressing ingredients and pour over the salad. Toss well and serve straight away.

# Italian Antipasti

My favourite place to hang out in Rome was a bar along the Tiber that offered a full table of antipasti for free, if you just bought a glass of wine first. As I was an impoverished student, my dinner was often their antipasti. I spent countless evenings sitting on the piazza outside the bar with friends, drinking wine and eating a whole plate of simple but show-stopping Italian starters.

Whenever the mint and ricotta-stuffed tomatoes made an appearance on that table, I was there to shamelessly fill my plate. The gorgeous shaved raw beet carpaccio here is a modern interpretation of an antipasti dish. The beets have a sweet, slightly nutty flavour with a bit of a sting. If you can't find the beautiful striped chioggia beets, replace them with regular red ones. — *David*

## Chioggia Beet Carpaccio

*4 raw chioggia beets, peeled*
*2 handfuls rocket*
*4 tbsp lemon juice*
*2 tbsp cold-pressed olive oil*
*4 tbsp raw pine nuts (pine kernels), toasted*
*1 small piece Parmesan cheese, shaved*

Slice the beets as thinly as you can, using a mandolin or a sharp knife. Arrange on a serving plate. Add the rocket and drizzle with lemon juice and olive oil. Toast the pine nuts in a frying pan over a very low heat. Scatter them over, add some shaved Parmesan cheese and serve.

## Mint & Ricotta Stuffed Cherry Tomatoes

*500 g (1 lb 2 oz) ripe cherry tomatoes*
*5 sprigs of mint, leaves picked*
*200 g (2 oz/scant 1 cup) full-fat ricotta cheese*
*sea salt and freshly ground black pepper*
*4 tbsp lemon juice*

Cut the tops off the tomatoes and discard them. Use a small spoon to remove the juicy seeds from the tomatoes and discard those too.

Chop most of the mint, reserving a few whole leaves for garnish. Stir the chopped mint into the ricotta cheese with a little salt and pepper and the lemon juice. Taste and adjust the seasoning. Fill the tomatoes with the ricotta cheese using a teaspoon, arrange on a serving plate and garnish with the reserved mint leaves.

# Sweet Vietnamese Cucumber Salad

When our daughter was nine months old, we spent two weeks in a tiny bungalow on the Vietnamese island Phu Quoc, without any hot water and with only three hours of electricity each day. We didn't fully realize what we had got ourselves into until we arrived there, and as large spiders climbed our mosquito net at night and scorpions crawled outside our door (true story), we started to question if we were taking our adventure a few steps too far. Looking back, those two weeks actually turned out to be the best part of the trip. We didn't get any animal bites (if you don't count the mosquitoes) and we got to eat some of the most fantastic and authentic Vietnamese food at the local wood-fired restaurant. Apart from summer rolls, noodle soups and stir-fries, we also had a variation of this delicious cucumber salad every night. It might look simple, but the sweet Vietnamese flavours make this salad the perfect accompaniment. A touch of honey, sesame oil, fresh coriander (cilantro), lime and chilli make the cucumber, radishes and pea sprouts dance in your mouth.

1 cucumber
5 radishes
1 handful coriander (cilantro), leaves picked and torn
1 handful pea sprouts
½ fresh chilli, seeded and very thinly sliced (or according to taste)
1 tsp sesame oil
juice of ½ lime
1 tsp clear honey (preferably unheated)
1 tbsp sesame seeds

Rinse the cucumber well in water and pat dry. Divide lengthwise and scoop out the seeds. Slice the cucumber and radishes thinly using a mandolin or a sharp knife and place in a bowl.

Add the coriander, pea sprouts and chilli and toss gently. Drizzle with sesame oil, lime juice and honey. Toss gently again. Sprinkle with the sesame seeds and serve.

# Quinoa Dolmades with Greek Salad

Thin vine leaves stuffed with grains and vegetables and wrapped in small parcels are common all over the Middle East and southern Europe. There is even a Nordic adaptation made with cabbage leaves, but here we have been inspired by the Greek version. It has always been one of my favourite savoury snacks to enjoy when travelling around the Greek islands. Once you learn the method, it is easy to replace any ingredients in the filling. We tried a rice version and also one with millet, but got most fond of this quinoa and fennel-stuffed edition. Eat them as snacks or serve them with a salad to turn them into a full meal. You can buy vacuum packs and jars of vine leaves, preserved in brine, in specialist food stores and some supermarkets. Alternatively, you can use freshly picked ones. Simply blanch in boiling water for 2–3 minutes to soften before use. — *David*

### Dolmas

50 g (2 oz/½ cup) uncooked quinoa, rinsed
250 ml (8½ fl oz/1 cup) water
a pinch of sea salt
¼ fennel bulb, finely chopped
1 onion, finely chopped
1 tomato, finely chopped
4 mint leaves, finely chopped
2 tbsp lemon juice
20 preserved vine leaves, drained
2 carrots, sliced lengthwise (or any root
   vegetables)
2 tbsp olive oil

### Salad

1 cucumber, seeded and sliced
200 g (7 oz/generous 1 cup) olives, drained
200 g (7 oz) Greek feta cheese, crumbled
2 handfuls cherry tomatoes, halved
4 sprigs of oregano
juice of ½ lemon
1 tbsp cold-pressed olive oil

Place the quinoa in a saucepan and add the measured water and a pinch of salt. Bring to the boil, reduce the heat immediately to medium-low and gently simmer for 15–20 minutes until tender and the water has been absorbed. Tip into a bowl and set aside to cool.

When cold, add all the remaining dolmas ingredients except the carrots and olive oil and toss gently to combine. Lay the vine leaves on a large surface with the ribs facing upwards. Place a spoonful of stuffing towards the stalk end of the leaf. Firmly roll the stalk end over the leaf, then tuck in the sides and roll up completely.

Prepare a saucepan with the sliced carrots in the bottom (to prevent the dolmas from burning while cooking). Pack the rolled dolmas seam-side down so they don't unravel, close together in layers in the saucepan. Place 2 plates (or other heavy object) on top of the dolmas to weigh them down. Pour over 120 ml (4 fl oz/½ cup) water or more to just cover. Cook for 20–30 minutes, adding the olive oil halfway through cooking. Remove the plates and drain off any excess liquid. Leave to cool to room temperature.

Meanwhile, divide the cucumber, olives, cheese and tomatoes among four serving plates. Add the dolmas, a sprig of oregano and a drizzle of lemon juice and olive oil to each plate and serve.

Tip: Vegans can just leave out the feta from the salad.

# SOUPS

# Harira Soup

You should have seen our daughter's eyes the first time we tried harira in Morocco. It was not so much the soup itself, but rather the dates by the side of the soup that got her attention. Dates are one of her absolute favourite things in the world and the thought of having them for dinner (with or without the soup) made her giggle with joy. They are actually one of the secrets behind this recipe. The sweet dates add roundness and, at the same time, increase the flavours of all the spices in this rich tomato and chickpea soup.

2 tbsp cold-pressed olive or coconut oil
1 onion
2 garlic cloves
2 large celery sticks
2 large carrots
1 tbsp ground ginger
1 tbsp ground paprika
1 tbsp ground turmeric
1 tbsp ground cumin
2 tbsp tomato purée
1 litre (34 fl oz/4¼ cups) water
  or vegetable stock
400 g (14 oz) can whole plum tomatoes
1 tbsp lemon juice, or more to taste
100 g (3½ oz/½ cup) dried chickpeas
  (garbanzos), soaked and cooked (or a 400 g/
  14 oz can, drained)

*To Serve*
a handful flat-leaf parsley, leaves picked
10 fresh soft dates, pitted (dried dates can
  be used, but fresh are more delicious)

Heat the oil in a large saucepan over a low to medium heat and sauté the onion, garlic, celery and carrots for about 5 minutes. Stir occasionally to make sure they don't brown too much. Add all four spices and stir well. Fry briefly, stirring, until they smell fragrant. Add the tomato purée, water or vegetable stock and tomatoes and simmer for 30 minutes. Add the lemon juice and more seasoning to taste.

Add the chickpeas and simmer for a further minute. Serve with plenty of fresh parsley and fresh dates on the side or cut into smaller pieces and place on the soup. It can be stored in the fridge for 3–5 days and freezes well.

# Paruppu Dhal Curry

The secret behind the most fragrant Sri Lankan lentil soup is to save half the spices until the soup is almost done, then stir-fry them in oil or ghee and pour the lentil soup over them for a more intense flavour. We learned this from a Sri Lankan woman who didn't speak a word of English. She had a daughter about the same age as Elsa and while they were playing hide and seek we got to spend an hour inside her kitchen, watching her cook and share some of her family recipes. Regardless of how thoroughly we scribble down every step and instruction, it is impossible to get exactly the same flavour once we come home from a trip to Asia. Local spices taste different and coconut milk is made fresh by grinding coconuts with a sharp tool. But when we tried this soup in our own kitchen in Stockholm, we were surprised by how authentic it tasted. Even though it is full of flavour it is also surprisingly mild, with warm tones of cinnamon. Curry leaves are available in Asian stores and some supermarkets.

100 g (3½ oz/½ cup) uncooked red lentils
10 fresh or dried curry leaves
1 small green chilli, seeded and finely chopped
1 onion, finely chopped
4 garlic cloves, finely chopped
2 tsp finely chopped fresh ginger
½ small cinnamon stick, broken into
    smaller pieces
1 tsp ground turmeric

1 tbsp curry powder
1 tsp sea salt
400 ml (14 fl oz) can full-fat
    coconut milk
450 ml (15 fl oz/2 cups) water
2 tbsp cold-pressed coconut oil or ghee

**To Serve**
wholegrain rice or naan bread

Soak the lentils in cold water for at least 10 minutes. Rinse well and drain. Place in a saucepan and add half each of the curry leaves, chilli, onion, garlic and ginger. Then add the cinnamon, turmeric, curry powder and salt. Pour the coconut milk and water into the pan, bring to the boil, reduce the heat and cook over low to medium heat for about 10–20 minutes, stirring occasionally, until the lentils are soft and the mixture is thick.

Pour the cooked dhal into a heatproof bowl. Heat the oil in the same saucepan and add the remaining curry leaves, chilli, onion, garlic and ginger. Cook for a couple of minutes until fragrant and slightly browned, stirring all the time to prevent them burning. Pour the cooked dhal back into the pot and bring back to a boil, stirring.

The dhal is now ready to be served but if you prefer it creamier, keep cooking until it is the desired consistency, stirring all the time. Serve with wholegrain rice or naan bread. The dhal can be stored in the fridge for up to 3–5 days.

# Vietnamese Pho

To get the most delicious Pho in Vietnam you should stay away from fancy restaurants. Instead, look for the most popular street corner vendors, as they make the best versions of this soup. The secret behind any good Pho is the stock. In Vietnam most stocks are made from big chunks of meat and bones, so we have improvised a bit to get a delicious vegetarian stock with the same breadth of flavour. One of the main ingredients in the stock is the dry-roasted or char-grilled star anise, which gives it that uniquely Vietnamese flavour. You can eat this at any time of the day – in Vietnam you would just as likely be served it for breakfast as dinner. Regardless of when you choose to eat it, don't forget to serve it with a load of fresh herbs, beansprouts and fresh lime to offset the richness of the soup.

*2 large onions, peeled and halved*
*10 cm (4 in) piece fresh ginger, peeled and sliced*
*4 cinnamon sticks*
*4 star anise*
*4 cloves*
*4 cardamom pods*
*1 tbsp coriander seeds*
*2 litres (68 fl oz/8 cups) vegetable stock/broth*
*1 tbsp organic, GMO-free soy sauce*
*2 large carrots, peeled and thickly sliced*
*½ fennel bulb, halved*
*250 g (9 oz) brown rice noodles or*
*buckwheat noodles*

*To Serve*
*350 g (12 oz) organic, GMO-free firm tofu,*
*sliced*
*1 head of bok choy, sliced*
*1 head of broccoli, cut into small florets*
*a large handful beansprouts*
*fresh herbs, such as Thai basil, coriander*
*(cilantro) and mint*
*2 limes, cut into wedges*
*2 tsp black or white sesame seeds*

Heat the oven to its hottest temperature. Place the onions and ginger slices on a baking tray and roast in the oven for about 5 minutes or until soft and with toasted edges.

Place the remaining spices in a heavy-based saucepan and dry-roast until aromatic, stirring to prevent them from burning. Add the vegetable stock, soy sauce, carrots, fennel and roast onion and ginger. Bring to the boil then reduce the heat, cover and simmer for 30 minutes. Pour the soup through a strainer to remove all the spices and vegetables, then tip the stock back into the pan and reheat. Meanwhile, cook the noodles according to the packet directions.

Prepare 4 serving bowls with cooked noodles, tofu slices, bok choy, broccoli, beansprouts, fresh herbs and lime wedges. When ready to serve, pour the hot soup stock over and sprinkle with sesame seeds.

# Chilled Avocado Soup

When we wrote on the blog that we were going to travel to California, we soon got an email from a reader inviting us to her family's avocado orchard. It was the first (and only) time we had picked avocados fresh from the trees and it was a truly memorable experience for me – but perhaps in some ways, one David would prefer to forget. While we were walking among their trees, they warned us (in a surprisingly relaxed manner) to look out for the rattlesnakes that were lurking on the ground. David is terrified of snakes and after that comment he lost interest in the avocado experience and focussed only on where he was putting his feet. We left the farm with more avocados than we could ever eat, and after two days of delicious sandwiches and guacamole, we started experimenting with warm and cold soups. Avocado soups are richer than almost any other soup, so smaller portions are usually enough. This version has tangy tones from yoghurt and lemon, heat from Tabasco and a Nordic twist with fresh dill. — *Luise*

*2 ripe avocados, halved and stone removed*
*finely grated zest of 1 lemon*
*4 tbsp lemon juice*
*½ small shallot, peeled*
*3 sprigs of dill, plus extra to garnish*
*3 sprigs of coriander (cilantro), leaves picked,*
  *or chive stalks, chopped, plus extra to garnish*
*4–8 drops of Tabasco or a pinch of ground*
  *cayenne*
*½ tsp sea salt*
*250 ml (8½ fl oz/1 cup) plain yoghurt*
  *(or use water or coconut water for a non*
  *dairy version)*

*To Serve*
*a drizzle of cold-pressed olive oil*
*60 g (2 oz/½ cup) pumpkin seeds,*
  *lightly toasted*

Scoop out the avocados with a spoon and add all the ingredients to a food processor or blender and purée until completely smooth. Add water little by little to thin to the required consistency, if necessary. Taste and adjust the flavours, then chill in the fridge.

Serve in glasses or bowls, topped with a splash of olive oil, toasted pumpkin seeds, chopped herbs and a sprig of dill. This soup doesn't keep very well, so make it the same day as serving.

# Sopa de Legumes Portuguese

On a recent trip to Portugal, I basically lived on vegetable soup and salads. Although the country has excellent fresh vegetables, it seems to focus all its dishes on fish or meat. I have rarely felt so limited when ordering at a restaurant as I did during that week. Luckily, almost all restaurants serve their own variety of creamy potato soup, which happens to be one of my favourite things in the world. So, even if I felt that I had very little to choose from, I was a pretty happy camper. We make our soup from a mix of potatoes, carrots and sweet potatoes – which gives it a very round and rich flavour – and top it with some fresh or cooked, dried broad (fava) beans for extra protein. — *David*

*1 tbsp cold-pressed olive or coconut oil*
*1 large onion, chopped*
*2 garlic cloves, chopped*
*10 fresh sage leaves, or 1 tsp dried*
*1 leek, sliced*
*2–3 potatoes (500 g /1 lb 2 oz,), peeled*
    *chopped*
*3 carrots (300 g/10½ oz), chopped*
*1 sweet potato or piece of pumpkin (200 g /7 oz),*
    *peeled and chopped*
*fine sea salt and freshly ground black pepper*
*2 tbsp lemon juice, or more to taste*
*250 g (9 oz/1½ cups) shelled fresh or*
    *100g (3½ oz/½ cup) dried broad (fava) beans,*
    *soaked and cooked*
*¼ small cabbage (100 g /3½ oz), chopped into*
    *2–3 pieces and separated into leaves*
*A little cold-pressed olive oil for drizzling*

Heat the oil in a large saucepan over a medium heat. Add the onion, garlic, sage and leek and cook for just a minute. Add the potatoes, carrots and sweet potato or pumpkin and stir. Cover with water and add some salt and pepper. Bring to the boil, cover, reduce the heat and cook until all the vegetables are tender. Remove from the heat and blend until smooth with a hand blender (or tip into a blender or food processor). Return to the heat and add lemon juice to taste. If using fresh broad beans, add to the soup, simmer for 4 minutes then add the cabbage and simmer for a minute or so more until the cabbage is just tender. If using cooked dried beans, add them with the cabbage. Taste and adjust the seasoning, if necessary. Serve in bowls with a drizzle of olive oil and freshly ground black pepper. The soup can be stored in the fridge for 3–5 days and freezes well.

# Zuppa di Ribollita

This rustic bread and bean soup sums up the things I love about the Italian way of cooking. Even if many Italians themselves are very fashionable, with high heels, sunglasses and expensive clothes, their cooking is the opposite; simple, rustic and down to earth. They don't need any fancy accessories to cook up the most delicious and beautiful meals. A few good-quality vegetables, fresh herbs and beans are quickly turned into a warm and comforting soup. In Tuscany it is common to add some day-old bread and a few slices of Parmesan to it, but if you are vegan or gluten intolerant they can be left out. — *David*

*2 tbsp cold-pressed olive oil, plus extra for serving*
*1 onion, chopped*
*4 garlic cloves, finely chopped*
*2 carrots, diced*
*a pinch of dried chilli flakes*
*10 sage leaves*
*a handful flat leaf parsley, leaves picked*
*1 tomato, diced*
*1 courgette (zucchini), halved lengthwise*
  *and sliced*
*300 g (10½ oz) cavolo nero green kale*
  *or Savoy cabbage*
*100g (3½ oz/½ cup) dried cannellini beans,*
  *soaked and cooked (or a 400g/14 oz can,*
  *drained)*
*about 1 litre (34 fl oz/4 cups) vegetable*
  *stock or water*
*sea salt and freshly ground pepper, to taste*

*To Serve*
*4 slices wholegrain sourdough bread, cubed*
*a piece of Parmesan cheese, shaved*

Heat the oil in a saucepan. Add the onion, garlic, carrots, chilli and sage and cook over a low heat for 20 minutes until softened but not browned. Add the parsley, tomato and courgette and cook for a couple of minutes. Add the cavolo nero and beans and cover with stock or water. Bring to the boil, reduce the heat and simmer for 30 minutes. Season to taste. The soup should be the consistency of a thick stew with a little broth. Serve in bowls and arrange bread cubes, shaved Parmesan cheese and a drizzle of olive oil over each.

# DINNERS

# Baked Aubergine Rolls

The Italian tradition of wrapping thinly sliced meat around a vegetable, fruit or cheese filling – *involtini* – doesn't have to be a dish exclusive to meat-eaters. The idea works just as well with thinly sliced aubergines (eggplants) or courgettes (zucchini). You could replace the millet with rice or quinoa in the filling – just make sure to include lots of fresh herbs, olives, capers, pine nuts (pine kernels) and pecorino. The tomato sauce is very basic, but fine for its purpose as most of the flavour comes from the filling. We often make this dish when we have guests coming over. The different preparation steps are great to do in groups.

*Simple Tomato Sauce*
*1 tbsp cold-pressed olive or coconut oil, or ghee*
*2 garlic cloves, crushed*
*2 x 400 g (14 oz) cans whole plum tomatoes*
*sea salt and freshly ground black pepper*

*Aubergines*
*2 large aubergines (eggplants)*
*2 tbsp cold-pressed olive oil*
*½ tsp coarse sea salt*

*Millet & Basil Filling*
*200 g (7 oz/1 cup) uncooked millet or quinoa*
*450 ml (15 fl oz/2 cups) water*

*1 handful basil leaves, finely chopped*
*  plus extra for serving*
*1 garlic clove, finely chopped*
*4 tbsp grated Pecorino or Parmesan,*
*  plus extra for serving*
*30 g (1 oz/¼ cup) pine nuts (pine kernels),*
*  coarsely chopped, plus extra for serving*
*20 olives, pitted and coarsely chopped*
*2 tbsp pickled capers, drained and crushed*
*juice of 1 lemon*
*sea salt and freshly ground black pepper*
*2 eggs*

*To Serve*
*a green salad*

Make the tomato sauce. Heat the oil in a saucepan, add the crushed garlic cloves and sauté for a moment. Add the canned tomatoes, salt and pepper, bring to the boil, reduce the heat and simmer gently for 20–30 minutes until pulpy.

Preheat the oven to 200°C (400°F/Gas 6). Slice the aubergines lengthwise into thin slices. Place on a grill rack in a baking tin. Use a pastry brush to brush them lightly with oil on both sides. Sprinkle with salt and roast in the oven until soft and browned on the edges, about 10 minutes. Keep an eye on them, they burn easily and will then be difficult to roll. Leave the oven on.

Meanwhile, rinse the millet in a sieve with boiling water. Drain well then place it in a saucepan and add the measured water. Bring to the boil, reduce the heat immediately and simmer gently for 10 minutes. Remove from the heat and set aside covered for a further 10 minutes.

Place the cooked millet in a large mixing bowl. Add all the filling ingredients, except the eggs, and mix well. Then add the eggs and combine. Place the grilled aubergine, one by one, in front of you with the largest end towards you. Add a couple of spoonfuls of the filling and roll upwards, away from you. Place the rolls in a baking dish in lines, ends down. Pour the tomato sauce over and bake for 15–20 minutes. Remove from the oven and garnish with the remaining grated cheese, pine nuts and fresh basil.

Serve with a green salad.

# No Noodle Pad Thai

This popular Thai dish has been cooked regularly in our kitchen ever since we first tried it in Bangkok. The first time we made it at home, we stayed true to the original recipe by stir-frying rice noodles in a sweet and a slightly spicy sauce, but through the years, it has slowly transformed into something new. Instead of stir-frying rice noodles, we now simply peel a daikon radish (courgette/zucchini also works fine) into thin strips that we toss with carrot strands, tofu and fresh herbs and cover with a peanut butter and lime dressing. Even though we have changed both cooking method and ingredients, it still has that wonderful flavour combination of sweet, nutty, tangy and a little spicy and the experience is light, fresh and, in our opinion, even tastier.

1 daikon radish, peeled or courgette (zucchini)
4 carrots, peeled
450 g (1 lb/4 cups) mung bean sprouts
4 spring onions (scallions), finely sliced
350 g (12 oz) organic, GMO-free firm tofu,
  cut in quarters
1 small handful coriander (cilantro) leaves,
  chopped, plus extra for serving
2 tbsp black sesame seeds, plus extra for serving
4 slices of lime, to serve

**Peanut Sauce**
125 g (4 oz/½ cup) peanut butter (adjust to allergies
  by choosing a different seed or nut butter)
4 tbsp lime juice
2 tbsp clear honey, preferably unheated
2 tbsp organic, GMO-free tamari or soy sauce
1 pinch ground cayenne pepper or more to taste
2 tsp grated fresh ginger
about 3 tbsp water, to thin

Use a julienne peeler, mandoline or spiralizer (or even a potato peeler) to create noodles from the daikon and carrots. Place in a bowl and add the mung bean sprouts and onions. Add the tofu, coriander and sesame seeds to the noodles and mix. Stir together all the sauce ingredients in a separate bowl, add more water if needed. Taste and adjust the seasoning. Pour over the vegetables and toss to combine using your hands. Make sure that every single strand is covered in dressing. Serve with a slice of lime, chopped coriander and sesame seeds on top. If making ahead, store the salad and peanut sauce in 2 separate containers. They can be stored in the fridge for a couple of days.

SERVES 4 / V / GF

# Baked Mushroom with Orange & Quinoa Tabbouleh

The parsley-packed tabbouleh salad is served as a side all across the Middle East and North Africa. It is one of the most flavourful salads we know, so in our home we often put it to better use than just serving it as a side dish. With the addition of orange, cinnamon and quinoa and paired with earthy-tasting baked Portobello mushrooms, it is a great dish during holiday celebrations. Bake the mushrooms until soft and juicy, pile tabbouleh in high stacks on them and top with pomegranate seeds. Not only is this dish delicious, it looks pretty stunning too.

4 Portobello mushrooms
2 tbsp cold-pressed olive oil
1 pomegranate, seeds scooped out and separated

**Tabbouleh Salad**
100 g (3½ oz/½ cup) quinoa
250 ml (8½ fl oz/1 cup) water
sea salt and freshly ground black pepper
4 large bunches parsley, finely chopped
1 large bunch mint, finely chopped
1 small orange, peeled and finely sliced
½ red onion, finely sliced
juice of ½ lemon
½ tsp ground cinnamon

Preheat the oven to 180ºC (350ºF/Gas 4). Clean the mushrooms and discard the stalks. Place the mushroom caps upside down in a baking dish. Drizzle with olive oil and bake for 15 minutes or until soft and juicy. Meanwhile rinse the quinoa in a sieve, then drain. Place in a saucepan and add the measured water and a pinch of sea salt. Bring to the boil, reduce the heat immediately and simmer gently for 15–20 minutes. Leave to cool slightly then mix together all the ingredients for the tabbouleh in a bowl. Let the mushrooms cool off slightly. Stack the tabbouleh high on top of the mushrooms, sprinkle with pomegranate seeds and serve. If making ahead, store the tabbouleh in an airtight container in the fridge for up to 3–5 days.

# Sweet Potato Gnocchi with Kale Pesto

I tried many different sorts of gnocchi when living in Italy, but I'll always remember a particular occasion. The restaurant was run by an old woman with a beautifully wrinkled face. Her family rushed between the tables, asking for personal preferences, and then returned to her so she could decide everyone's menu. '*Si preferisce bistecca o pollo stasera?*' ('Do you prefer steak or chicken tonight?) I was asked. '*Mi dispiace, ma io non mangio carne*' ('Sorry, but I don't eat meat'). The young man looked surprised and then waved his grandmother to our table to confront me. She explained that they had the best meat in Rome and she was certain I would love it. I could at least choose the chicken. I stood firm and, disappointed, she said she would make something simple for me. Her homemade potato dumplings in pesto might have been the simplest dish in her kitchen, but they were heaven to me. I am sure that her version wasn't gluten-free or made from sweet potatoes, but ours are. They have a sweet and slightly nutty flavour, a pretty orange colour and a wonderfully soft texture. — *David*

*Gnocchi*
1 sweet potato (about 250 g/9 oz)
1 egg, beaten
½ tsp sea salt
¼ teaspoon freshly grated nutmeg
60 g (2 oz/½ cup) quinoa flour
80 g (3 oz/½ cup) rice flour
2 tbsp potato flour, cornflour (cornstarch)
   or arrowroot
olive oil, for drizzling

*Kale & Hazelnut Pesto*
75 g (2½ oz/½ cup) hazelnuts (filberts)
100 g (3½ oz) kale, stems removed
1 handful basil leaves
4 tbsp freshly grated Pecorino cheese
juice of ½ lemon
90 ml (3 fl oz/⅓ cup) cold-pressed olive oil

Preheat the oven to 220°C (425°F/Gas 7). Cut the sweet potato in half and place on a baking sheet, cut side down. Roast on the centre shelf for about 30 minutes, or until tender.

While the sweet potato cooks, make the pesto. Toast the hazelnuts in a dry frying pan over a medium-low heat until golden and the skins have split. Rub between a rough tea towel to help get the peel off. Place in a food processor together with the rest of the ingredients. Run at high speed until the desired consistency is reached, adding a splash of water if needed.

When the sweet potato is cooked, leave until it is cool enough to handle then scoop out the flesh and mash it with a fork in a wide bowl. Stir in the egg, salt and nutmeg and mix until combined. Sift together the flours and add two-thirds to the sweet potato. Stir

together quickly until combined. Dust a work surface with some of the remaining flour and turn the dough onto it. Knead the dough very gently with your hands, adding more flour if needed. The dough should be moist but not sticky. Divide the dough into four portions. Dust with more flour and roll one portion into a long log, 1 cm (½ in) wide. Use a knife or metal pastry scraper to cut the log into 2.5 cm (1 in) pillows. To shape the gnocchi, dust a fork with flour, place a piece of gnocchi with the cut side towards the back of the fork, press lightly with the fork and roll it down to create the tiny ridges. Alternatively, simply press the fork into each gnocchi – they will be more square, but will still taste good. Repeat with the remaining portions.

Bring a large saucepan of salted water to the boil over a medium-

high heat. Carefully drop in about 15 gnocchi. When they float up to the surface (after about a minute), wait 30 seconds and then fish them out of the water with a slotted spoon. Keep warm while cooking the remaining batches of gnocchi. Serve them warm with a few spoonfuls of Kale & Hazelnut Pesto (or whatever you prefer) and a drizzle of olive oil. You can also save the gnocchi for later and give them a quick fry in a buttered skillet together with vegetables or any kind of sauce.

Tip: Kale is one of the healthiest vegetables around and you want to eat it on a regular basis. A simple trick to get more kale into your and your kids diet is to blend it up in pestos, dressings or even in smoothies. That way it's easier to digest and you'll eat superfood without even noticing it.

DINNERS

# Holiday Stuffed Pumpkins

A couple of years ago, we were in the USA during Thanksgiving. It is not something we celebrate in Scandinavia, so we weren't prepared for the hype that surrounds this American holiday. We were invited to the home of a distant relative of David. They wanted to give us a proper celebration and had prepared an impressive table of sweet pies, Brussels sprout salad, potatoes, condiments and... the largest turkey we had ever seen. Unfortunately, David had forgotten to tell them the small detail that he was a vegetarian. He couldn't bear disappointing his well-meaning relatives and looked at me with panic in his eyes. Throughout that evening he carefully smuggled all his pieces of turkey on to my plate, while digging in on the side dishes. After that experience, we started to think that vegetarians need their own Thanksgiving dish, instead of always being left with the sides. The stuffed pumpkins are our version of a centrepiece. They are filled with delicious autumn vegetables, pistachio nuts, raisins and cinnamon. Here we have used smaller Hokkaido pumpkins, but a larger Muscat pumpkin also works well – it just needs longer cooking time. — *Luise*

400 g (14 oz/2 cups) wholegrain rice (any colour will work)
1.2 litres (40 fl oz/5 cups) water
2 Hokkaido pumpkins
2 tbsp cold-pressed coconut or olive oil (reserve 1 tbsp for rubbing the pumpkins)
2 large onions, finely chopped
2 handful mushrooms of choice, coarsely chopped

6 kale leaves (any type will work), thick stalks removed, coarsely chopped
100 g (3½ oz/⅔ cup) shelled pistachio nuts, coarsely chopped
5 sprigs of mint, leaves picked and chopped
3 tbsp raisins
½ tsp ground cinnamon
150 g (5 oz) feta cheese, crumbled

Rinse and drain the rice. Place in a saucepan together with the water and bring to the boil. Reduce the heat and cover with a lid. Simmer gently for about 40 minutes until tender.

Meanwhile, prepare the pumpkins. Cut a lid out of the top of each one, then scoop out the seeds and discard. Rub the insides with oil and set aside.

Preheat the oven to 200°C (400°F/Gas 6). Heat 1 tablespoon oil in a large frying pan and fry the onions, mushrooms and kale over a medium-low heat until soft and cooked, but not brown. Remove from the heat, add the pistachios, mint, raisins and cinnamon and stir well. Add the cooked rice and crumbled feta cheese and toss to combine. Spoon the stuffing into the greased pumpkins, put the 'lids' back on and bake in the oven for 20–30 minutes or until the skin is browned and bubbly. Check with a knife to see if the pumpkin flesh is soft. Serve hot. Leftovers can be stored in the fridge for 3–5 days.

# Chermoula Baked Cauliflower

Chermoula is a marinade that is most commonly used as a seasoning for fish and meat in Morocco. It has an intense taste of fresh herbs, garlic, lemon and saffron and it seemed unfair to us that vegetarians often miss out on such a flavour-booster. Luise came up with the idea of rubbing it into a whole cauliflower head and baking until the cauliflower is all golden and crusty on the outside and soft and buttery on the inside. Here we have served it with a fresh and flavourful fattoush salad and some flatbreads (we like to eat the flatbreads alongside the fattoush rather than tearing them up and adding them to it, as is often done). A simple green salad instead would be sufficient alternative. — *David*

2 garlic cloves
2 tsp ground cumin
2 tsp ground coriander
1 tsp dried chilli flakes
1 tsp ground paprika
1 tsp ground ginger or grated fresh ginger
¼ tsp ground saffron (or a pinch of saffron strands)
½ tsp sea salt
juice of 1 small lemon
3 tbsp cold-pressed olive or coconut oil, or ghee
1 cauliflower

Mash the garlic cloves into small pieces with the back of a knife and remove the skin. Place in a bowl, along with the rest of the ingredients except the cauliflower. Stir to combine. Prepare the cauliflower by cutting off and discarding the green leaves and placing the white head in a baking dish. Pour the chermoula marinade over and rub it all over the cauliflower using your hands. Leave to marinate for at least 1 hour or up to 12 hours.

Preheat the oven to 200°C (400°F/Gas 6). Bake the cauliflower for 30–40 minutes. The baking time depends on the oven and the size of the cauliflower. Check with a sharp knife to see if it is tender right through. Serve warm.

# Fattoush salad

2 cucumbers, sliced
500 g (1 lb 2 oz) cherry tomatoes, halved (a mixture of red and yellow is good)
1 large handful radishes, thinly sliced
1 red onion, sliced
30 g (1 oz/1 cup) coarsely chopped flat-leaf parsley
15 g (½ oz/½ cup) coarsely chopped mint leaves
1 cos (romaine) lettuce, torn in pieces

*Dressing*
60 ml (2 fl oz/¼cup) cold-pressed olive oil
60 ml (2 fl oz/¼ cup) lemon juice
2 tbsp ground sumac
1 tbsp pomegranate molasses or honey
2 garlic cloves, crushed
1 tbsp apple cider vinegar

*To Serve*
raw seed crackers or flatbreads
plain yoghurt, optional

Put all the prepared vegetables and herbs in a large bowl. Whisk together the dressing ingredients, pour over the salad and toss it well.

Serve with raw seed crackers or flatbreads and plain yoghurt.

# Lemongrass, Aubergine & Brussels Sprout Curry

This is a simple green Thai curry made from scratch, with a distinct tang of lemongrass, a sweet apple tone and a soft touch of coconut milk. It is inspired by one of the many curries we tried in Thailand. There they use small aubergines (eggplants) cut in half, but since they are difficult to find in Scandinavia we use the larger sort. If Brussels sprouts aren't in season, you can replace them with any kind of cabbage, cut into bite-sized chunks.

*2 tbsp cold-pressed coconut or olive oil*
*4 garlic cloves, finely chopped*
*2.5 cm (1 in) piece fresh ginger, finely chopped*
*2 lemongrass stalks, crushed and very finely chopped*
*½ tsp dried chilli flakes*
*2 tsp ground turmeric or grated fresh tumeric*
*1 tsp mustard seeds, ground in a mortar*
*1 aubergine (eggplant), cut in small wedges*
*2 small apples, peeled, cored and cut in cubes*
*250 ml (8½ fl oz/1 cup) water*
*1 tbsp apple cider vinegar*
*400 ml (14 fl oz) can full-fat coconut milk*
*300 g (10½ oz) Brussels sprouts, cut in half*
*1 tsp fine sea salt*

*To Serve*
*black rice*
*1 generous handful of Thai basil and coriander (cilantro) leaves*

Heat the oil in a large saucepan over a medium heat. Add the garlic and all the spices and reduce the heat. Sauté for a couple of minutes and stirring constantly to ensure they do not burn. Add the aubergine wedges one by one making sure all wedges get soaked in the spicy oil. Then add the apple, water and apple cider vinegar, cover with a lid and cook for 15–20 minutes or until aubergine wedges are tender. Add the coconut milk, Brussels sprouts and sea salt to the curry and gently simmer for about 10 more minutes. Stir in the Thai basil and coriander and serve with black rice and some salad on the side. Leftovers can be stored in the fridge for 3–5 days.

# Chocolate Bean Chilli with Walnuts

In the Mexican beach town Playa del Carmen, we stumbled upon a very special little restaurant that used chocolate in all the dishes on their menu. Intrigued by the idea, we decided to try some of the more odd items, such as chocolate salad, chocolate ceviche and chocolate lasagne. From that experience we learned that everything doesn't taste better with chocolate (their desserts were amazing, though). One Mexican dish that is great with chocolate is their bean chilli, or mole. Our recipe is something of a mix between the Mexican mole and a chilli con carne. We have added walnuts to give it some crunch. You can give this dish even more depth by replacing 120 ml (4 fl oz/½ cup) water with red wine.

*2 tbsp cold-pressed coconut or olive oil, or ghee*
*1 large yellow onion, finely chopped*
*2 garlic cloves, finely chopped*
*2 tsp cumin seeds or 1 tsp ground cumin*
*1 fresh chilli, deseeded and minced*
*(more if you like it hot)*
*1 tsp ground paprika*
*1 tsp dried oregano*
*1 red and 1 yellow (bell) pepper,*
*seeded and finely chopped*
*1 carrot, finely chopped*
*2 corn cobs (kernels cut off) or 150 g (5 oz/1 cup)*
*thawed frozen corn*
*2 large celery sticks (use leaves too), finely sliced*
*150 g (5 oz/1½ cups) walnuts, very finely*
*chopped*

*300 g (10½ oz/1½ cups) dried mixed beans,*
*such as kidney, black and adzuki, black-eye or borlotti,*
*soaked and cooked,(or 3 x 400g/14 oz cans cooked*
*mixed pulses, drained)*
*2 x 400 g (14 oz) cans whole plum tomatoes*
*250 ml (8 ½ fl oz/1 cup) water*
*2 tsp sea salt and freshly ground black pepper*
*60 g (2 oz) 80% minimum cacao dark chocolate,*
*broken into pieces*

*To Serve*
*120 ml (4 fl oz/½ cup) plain yoghurt, or a*
*vegan alternative*
*1 large handful coriander (cilantro) leaves, coarsely*
*chopped*
*4 corn tortillas, toasted*

Heat the oil in a large heavy-based saucepan or casserole (Dutch oven) over a medium heat. Add the onion, garlic, cumin, chilli, paprika and oregano and cook for a couple of minutes, stirring occasionally, until the spices smell fragrant and the onions are soft but not browned. Add the peppers, carrot, corn and celery, cook for another couple of minutes. Add the walnuts, beans, tomatoes, water and salt, bring to the boil, then reduce the heat and simmer for 20 minutes. Now add the chocolate, stir in carefully and cook for another couple of minutes. Taste and season with sea salt and freshly ground pepper. Serve in bowls, garnished with a dollop of yoghurt and chopped coriander with toasted corn tortillas on the side. Store any leftover in the fridge for 3–5 days.

# Berber Tagine

One of our goals when we visited Marrakech last year was to learn how to cook a tagine properly; we had been doing our own versions for years, which we featured in our last book. This time we got to visit a Moroccan mother's home and peek into her kitchen while she cooked a tagine. Fouzia's method was more complicated than we had anticipated, with many of the vegetables prepared separately and then assembled in the tagine towards the end. It tasted perfect, though – exactly the flavours we were aiming for. Our version of her recipe is simpler, allowing all the vegetables to slow-cook simultaneously in the tagine. One of the secrets to success is to use slightly more spices than you're comfortable with and to add a bit of saffron too.

*90 ml (3 fl oz/⅓ cup) cold-pressed olive oil*
*  or melted ghee, plus a little for frying*
*1 tsp ground ginger*
*1 tsp ground paprika*
*½ tsp ground black pepper or cayenne pepper*
*1 tsp ground turmeric*
*¼ tsp ground saffron or a pinch of saffron strands*
*1 tsp dried thyme*
*2 onions, finely chopped*
*2 large tomatoes, finely chopped*
*4 carrots, sliced lengthwise*
*4 parsnip or turnips, sliced lengthwise*

*2 sweet potatoes, sliced lengthwise*
*1 courgette (zucchini), sliced lengthwise*
*1 handful golden or brown raisins*
*400 ml (13 fl oz/1½ cups) water*
*1 handful golden or brown raisins*
*1 onion, sliced*
*1 tomato, sliced*
*1 handful parsley leaves, torn*

*To Serve*
*green salad*
*bread, quinoa or millet*

**TO COOK IN A TAGINE OR CLAY POT**

Soak the tagine for at least 1 hour, then drain. Mix the oil, spices and thyme in a bowl. Pour half into the bottom of the tagine, add the onions and tomatoes and toss to combine. Arrange the sliced vegetables in a circle, starting with the carrots, then the parsnips, sweet potatoes and courgette. Add the water to the remaining spice mixture, mix and pour over the vegetables. Sprinkle with raisins and cover with the tagine lid. Place in a cold oven and turn the heat to 160°C (325°F/Gas 3) and cook for 2 hours, checking once, or at most twice, to see if more water is needed. Turn off the heat and leave to stand in the oven for 30 minutes.

Heat a little oil or ghee in a frying pan and fry the onion and tomato slices briefly to soften. When ready to serve, arrange on top of the vegetables in the tagine and scatter the parsley over.

**TO COOK IN A HEAVY-BASED SAUCEPAN**

Heat the oil in the saucepan over a medium heat. Add the spices, thyme and chopped onions and tomatoes and cook until soft but not browned. Add all the vegetables and stir to coat in spices. Add water to barely cover the vegetables. Top with the raisins, bring to the boil, reduce the heat to low and simmer gently for 30–40 minutes or until completely tender. Fry the onion and tomato slices in a little oil or ghee in a frying pan until softened, place on top of the vegetables and scatter the parsley over. Serve the tagine with a green salad and bread, quinoa or millet.

# Creamy Polenta with Mushrooms & Artichoke

This recipe is inspired by a dish we had at a wonderful hole-in-the-wall restaurant that we have managed to visit only once, somewhere in the Born district of Barcelona. We have gone half a dozen times to try to find it again, but with no luck: the winding streets always leave us lost and confused. As far as we can remember, their polenta was firmer, almost like a cake, and the dish was served as a starter. Instead, we have made the polenta soft and creamy. To get the right consistency we use a similar method to preparing risotto, with liquid added in small portions as it cooks. We top it with fragrant garlic mushrooms, artichoke hearts and a slice or two of goats' cheese.

*Polenta*
*1.5 litres (50 fl oz/6 cups) water*
*150 g (5 oz/1 cup) coarse-ground polenta*
*2 tsp fine sea salt, or to taste*
*4 tbsp cold-pressed olive oil or ghee*
   *or 50 g (2 oz/½ stick) butter*

*Topping*
*2 garlic cloves, crushed*
*9 oz (250 g) crimini (button chestnut)*
   *mushrooms*
*150 g (5 oz) marinated artichoke hearts,*
   *drained*
*4 sprigs of thyme, leaves picked*
*4–8 slices goats' cheese, depending on the sizes*
   *of the cheese*
*cold-pressed olive oil for drizzling*

Place 1 litre (34 fl oz/4¼ cups) water in a heavy-based saucepan and bring to a simmer. Heat the remaining measured water in a kettle or separate saucepan. Add the polenta and salt to the first saucepan and stir to combine. Immediately reduce the heat to a very low simmer and stir frequently until the water has been absorbed. Continue to simmer, adding a little more water about every 5 minutes or so, for 45 minutes until the mixture is thick and creamy and pulls away from the sides of the saucepan. Stir in half the olive oil, ghee or butter.

Heat the remaining oil, ghee or butter in a separate saucepan over a medium heat. Add the garlic and mushrooms and cook for a couple of minutes. Then add the artichoke hearts and thyme and cook for another couple of minutes until everything is tender and juicy. Move to the side of the pan and cook the slices of cheese for no more than a minute on each side.

Serve the creamy polenta on plates and top with a few spoonfuls of mushroom and artichokes, a slice of warm goats' cheese and a drizzle of olive oil.

# Whole Egg Flower Curry

We devour eggs in all forms, from our morning scrambles to our dessert crêpes. If you were to pair them with another thing that is close to our heart – Indian cuisine – this is the dish you would end up with. The flavourful egg curry is a simple and comforting dish that can be found all across India. Tradition says that all egg curries should be made with hard-boiled eggs, but we much prefer cracking them right into the sauce and letting them slowly cook until just firm. The eggs end up with a charming, frilly, flower-like appearance. This dish oozes warm Indian spices and a fresh zing of mint.

Serve with some naan breads or chapattis to soak up the sauce, or black rice, if you are serving a hungry crowd. We like to use some red perilla – a form of mint – as well as the usual green leaves for garnish.

2 tbsp ghee or cold-pressed coconut oil
½ tsp yellow mustard seeds
1 onion, finely chopped
2 garlic cloves, finely chopped
1 tsp finely chopped fresh ginger
½ tsp chilli powder, or to taste
½ tsp ground turmeric
1 tsp garam masala
120 ml (4 fl oz/½ cup) water
2 x 400 g (14 oz) cans chopped tomatoes
1 tsp sea salt
4 sprigs fresh mint, leaves picked and coarsely
   chopped
300 g (10½ oz/2 cups) fresh shelled or thawed
   frozen peas
4 tbsp coconut cream (the firm top layer of
   coconut milk)
6 eggs
a few nigella seeds (optional)

**To Serve**
a side salad
wholegrain rice, chapatis or naan
   breads, optional

Heat the ghee in a frying pan over medium heat, add the mustard seeds and cook for a minute or until they start to pop. Add the onion, garlic and ginger and cook until soft and the mixture smells fragrant. Add the chilli, turmeric and garam masala, stir, and simmer for about 30 seconds. Add the water and cook for about 5 minutes.

Add the tomatoes and sea salt, then cover and simmer for 20 minutes. Stir in half the mint, the peas and coconut cream. Make 6 small indentations in the sauce for the eggs and carefully crack the eggs into them. Cover the pan with a lid and simmer gently for 5 minutes, or until the egg whites have set. Scatter with the remaining mint and a few nigella seeds, if using, and serve with a side salad, wholegrain rice, chapatis or naan breads.

# Mushroom & Tofu Dumplings

'*Wo bu chi rou*,' I said with my best Chinese accent, but all I got back was shaking heads. 'I am a vegetarian,' I said slowly, as if that would help. Still nothing.

A very kind blog reader had sent us a list of Chinese phrases for our trip to Beijing, but unfortunately none of them helped. Consequently, our five days in China weren't as filled with delicious food as we had hoped. The only exception was when we found a dumpling restaurant with an owner who finally understood the word 'vegetarian'. He came in with a full tray of shiitake-filled dumplings served with an ocean of different sauces and condiments. It was heaven. The easiest way to make gluten-free dumplings is to use rice paper wrappers instead of dumpling dough. They are very easy to handle and taste great. The rice paper dumplings can be steamed, fried or baked and the filling can of course be adapted to what you have available. — *David*

*a knob of cold-pressed coconut oil*
*1 onion, finely chopped*
*5 cm (2 in) piece fresh ginger, finely chopped*
*a large handful shiitake or oyster mushrooms,*
  *coarsely chopped*
*¼ cabbage, finely shredded*
*200 g (7 oz) organic, GMO-free firm tofu,*
  *crumbled*
*rice paper wrappers*

**Soy Dipping Sauce**
*2 tbsp organic, GMO-free soy sauce*
*2 tbsp water*

*1 tsp clear honey (preferably unheated)*
*1 tsp sesame seeds*
*a small piece of fresh chilli, thinly sliced*

**Vegetables**
*1 head of broccoli, cut into small florets*
*¾ cabbage, cut in wedges*
*1 bok choy or pak choi, cut in wedges*

**To Serve**
*Dried Plum Sauce (see page 243)*

Heat the oil in a frying pan over a medium heat. Add the onion and ginger and cook for a few minutes until softened, but not browned. Add the remaining vegetables and cook for about 5 minutes until tender. Add the crumbled tofu and combine. Remove from the heat and set the filling aside.

To make the dumplings, first set a bowl of hot water on the work surface. Dip a sheet of rice paper in the hot water for a few seconds, just so you can form it, but not too soft, and place on a plate. Add a spoonful of filling in the centre of the soft rice paper and close the dumpling by twisting the rice paper together until it forms a twisted top. Make all the dumplings before steaming. Prepare the soy dipping sauce

by stirring together all the ingredients in a small bowl (and make the plum sauce, if not already made).

Steam the dumplings in a steaming basket or metal colander with a lid over a pan of simmering water for a couple of minutes. If you have tiered steaming baskets, steam the vegetables at the same time. If not, steam the dumplings, then keep warm, covered, while you steam the vegetables. If you are not serving the dumplings right away, you might want to place them on a piece of baking parchment in the steaming basket to prevent them from sticking to the bottom and breaking when lifted.

Serve with the 2 sauces.

# Stir Fried Red Rice

It is impossible to travel in Asia and not encounter a bowl of fried rice; it is on every menu in every country. If you are travelling with kids and find the curries too spicy for them, the fried rice is always a good and simple choice, at least in our family. At only nine months old, Elsa loved stuffing her face full of rice, vegetables and tofu. We make our version with wholegrain rice, which adds chewiness and earthy tones to the dish. One of the tricks to get the dish right is to give the vegetables only a quick turn in the pan, so they stay fresh and crisp. Another trick is to make sure that the cooked rice is completely dry before it is added to the pan – that way it doesn't make the dish soggy.

Stir-fried Rice is also a great way to use up any leftover rice or vegetables, as it is very easy to improvise and substitute ingredients. Add tofu or tempeh for extra protein.

200 g (7 oz/1 cup) red, brown or other
    wholegrain rice
500 ml (17 fl oz/2¼ cups) water
1 tbsp cold-pressed coconut or olive oil or ghee
1 large carrot, thinly sliced
1 large handful oyster mushrooms, sliced
2 spring onions (scallions), sliced
½ bok choy or a large handful of spinach,
    thinly sliced
sea salt and freshly ground black pepper
2 eggs, beaten

*To Serve*
60 g (2 oz/ ⅓ cup) raw cashew nuts
1 large handful fresh Thai basil leaves

Rinse the rice and place in a saucepan with the measured water. Bring to the boil, reduce the heat, cover and gently cook over a medium-low heat for 25–30 minutes. Drain the rice thoroughly and set aside for 10 minutes.

Heat the oil in a frying pan, add the vegetables and stir-fry for a couple of minutes. Season with sea salt and black pepper. Add the rice and fry for another minute. Add the beaten eggs and stir until scrambled. Scatter with cashew nuts and Thai basil leaves and serve.

# Vegan Sweet Potato & Aubergine Moussaka

I spent many summers boat-hopping around the Greek islands and vegetable moussaka was always a reliable dinner companion. This oily pasta-free Greek relative to the Italian lasagne is filled with lentils, which makes it a very nourishing dinner. Normally the moussaka is baked with enormous amounts of cheese on top, but we skipped that and went for a vegan béchamel instead. Our version has the same richness to it and makes for a most comforting meal.

*Layers*
*2 aubergines (eggplants), very thinly sliced*
*2 tbsp cold-pressed olive oil*
*sea salt*
*2 sweet potatoes, peeled and very thinly sliced*

*Lentil & Tomato Sauce*
*2 tbsp cold-pressed olive or coconut oil*
*1 large onion, finely chopped*
*2 garlic cloves, finely chopped*
*1 tsp ground cinnamon*
*2 tsp dried oregano*
*2 tbsp tomato purée (paste)*
*250 g (9 oz/1½ cups) green lentils, preferably*
  *presoaked for 1 hour or up to 8 hours*

*600 ml (20 fl oz/2½ cups) water*
*400 g (14 oz) can chopped tomatoes*
*1 tsp sea salt*

*Vegan Béchamel Sauce*
*2 tbsp cold-pressed olive oil, plus extra for*
  *drizzling, if necessary*
*4 tbsp chickpea flour or flour of your choice*
*2 cups unsweetened plant milk (almond milk,*
  *organic GMO-free soya milk, oat milk etc.)*
*¼ tsp freshly grated nutmeg*
*sea salt and freshly ground pepper*

*To Serve*
*micro greens or sprouts*

Preheat the oven to 200°C (400°F/Gas 6). Lay the aubergine slices on a grill rack in a baking tin and brush the tops with a very thin layer of oil. Sprinkle lightly with sea salt and roast in the oven until soft and lightly browned, about 10 minutes, depending on how thinly sliced they are. Place the prepared sweet potatoes in a bowl of cold water until ready for use to keep them fresh and moist.

Make the lentil and tomato sauce by heating the oil in a saucepan. Add the onion, garlic, cinnamon and oregano and fry until fragrant, stirring occasionally. Add the tomato purée and keep stirring until well mixed. Now add the lentils, water and tomatoes. Bring to the boil, reduce the heat to medium-low, cover and simmer for 30–40 minutes, until the lentils are soft and the sauce is 'dry'.

Make the béchamel sauce by heating the oil in a small saucepan over a medium-low heat. Add the flour and stir until thick and slightly browned. Whisking constantly, add half the milk, whisk, add the remaining milk and whisk until smooth. Add the nutmeg and season. Cook, whisking constantly, until the sauce comes to the boil and thickens.

Reduce the oven heat to 180°C (350°F/Gas 4). Arrange a third of the aubergine slices in the base of a fairly large baking dish. Top with half of the sweet potato slices and half of the lentil and tomato sauce. Repeat. Finish with the remaining aubergine slices and then pour the béchamel sauce over. Bake for 35–40 minutes. Test to see if the sweet potatoes are tender by inserting a sharp knife down through the centre. Remove from the oven and leave to cool for 30 minutes before serving. Drizzle some olive oil over it before serving if it looks a little dry.

# Chapter Six

# DRIPS & DROPS

# Sri Lankan Passion Fruit & Avocado Drink

Avocado and passion fruit might seem like an odd match, but they add creaminess and freshness to this smoothie that we were served as a welcome drink on one of our favourite home-stays in Sri Lanka. Today, passion fruit has become an essential addition to our juices and smoothies whenever we want a fresh and exotic twist.

½ avocado, stoned
3 large passion fruit, halved
2 thick slices pineapple, peeled and cubed
½ mango, peeled and flesh cut off stone
1 orange, peeled and segmented
4 ice cubes

Scoop the avocado flesh and passion fruit pulp into a blender. Add all the remaining ingredients and process until smooth. Add water to thin, if needed. Serve in glasses with straws. Drink immediately.

# Ice-cold Wheatgrass Morning Shooter

The photo of this wheatgrass shot was taken at a stall in the Union Square Green Market in New York – the very epicentre of the healthy-living hype. They, of course, squeeze their wheatgrass through a manual juicing machine and people line up to drink the not-so delicious but oh-so nutritious shot straight up. At home I have a slightly different way of preparing my wheatgrass shot. Even though it would be cool to have a wheatgrass juicer on our kitchen counter, there are about a dozen other kitchen appliances that are more important. Instead, we use dried wheatgrass powder that we mix up with lots of fresh lime and ginger for a much nicer flavour. — *Luise*

*2 limes*
*2.5 cm (1 in) fresh ginger*
*1 tsp wheatgrass powder or more to taste*

Place 2 shot glasses in the freezer for as much time as you have. Juice the limes and ginger in a juicer and pour into a jug. (Alternatively, squeeze the lime by hand and grate the ginger on a fine grater.) Add the wheatgrass powder and give it a really good stir. Remove the shot glasses from the freezer and pour the juice into them. Drink immediately. Cheers!

DRIPS & DROPS

# Green Yoga Smoothie

Layered smoothies are not only pretty but also more fun to drink since the flavour changes as you sip. It is also the only way to combine green vegetables with red berries without ending up with a nasty brown color. One of the unexpectedly best smoothie bars I have visited was on a beach just north of Barcelona. From a distance it looked like as if the dancing bartenders were shaking up cocktails, but instead they were mixing the most amazing juices and smoothies with fresh fruit, various superfoods and nut milks. — *Luise*

*1 ripe mango (about 250 g/9 oz), peeled and*
*   flesh cut off stone, discarded (thawed frozen*
*   is fine too)*
*juice of ½ lemon*
*2.5 cm (1 in) fresh ginger or ½ tsp ground*
*   ginger*
*2 handfuls leafy greens of your choice*
*   (spinach, kale, chard etc.)*
*2 tbsp hemp seeds*
*2 tsp barleygrass powder or grass powder of*
*   your choice (optional)*
*250 ml (8½ fl oz/1 cup) natural coconut*
*   water or unsweetened plant milk*
*1 large handful ice cubes*
*200 g (7 oz/1⅔ cups) fresh or thawed frozen*
*   raspberries, crushed*

Place all the ingredients except the raspberries in a high-speed blender and mix until smooth and creamy. Taste and adjust to your preference. Spoon the raspberries into 2 jars or glasses, pour the green smoothie over and serve with a spoon.

   Tip: Start with 1 teaspoon barleygrass powder per person and work your way up to 1 tablespoon.

# Sweet Cashew Milk

'Natural Plant Milkshake!' was written on a large white sign at the far end of the lane. We had made a stop at practically every farmer's market we passed on our trip down the American West Coast and this type of hippy sign was one of the reasons why. The owner of the sign poured us two glasses from a large pitcher and told us that this was his wife's secret recipe. No matter how much we pressed him, he wouldn't share the ingredients with us. It was one of the most delicious drinks we had ever tried and as soon as we had found ourselves a kitchen with a blender, we started experimenting with sweet plant milks. I am not sure if we got all the ingredients or amounts right, but this has the same balance of sweet, creamy and refreshing elements. Add more or less water depending on how rich you like it.

*225 g ( 8 oz/1½ cups) raw cashew nuts*
*750 ml (25 fl oz/3 cups) chilled water, preferably*
  *filtered*
*½ tsp each of ground vanilla or vanilla extract,*
  *cinnamon, or cardamom*
*a pinch of coarse sea salt*
*6 fresh soft dates, pitted*

Cover the cashew nuts with water and soak for about 8 hours or as long as you have. Drain and place in a blender with the measured water and the remaining ingredients. Blend until smooth and creamy. Serve immediately or store for up to 3 days in the fridge.

# Mexican Cacao, Rice & Amaranth Drink

We had a drink similar to this in a tiny restaurant along the Yucatán coastline in Mexico. It is an ice-cold and fresh version of hot chocolate, with a hint of sweetness from the rice milk and cinnamon, softness and protein from the amaranth and a little bitterness from the cacao. It is super simple to make and the perfect drink on warm days or as a quick energy boost. You can buy puffed amaranth in health food stores and some large supermarkets.

*500 ml (17 fl oz/2¼ cups) unsweetened rice milk
   or milk of your choice*
*3 tbsp puffed amaranth*
*2 tsp organic cacao or cocoa powder, plus extra
   for sprinkling*
*½ tsp ground cinnamon*
*4 ice cubes*

Place all the ingredients in a blender and mix on high speed until smooth. Pour into two bowls or large glasses. Sprinkle with puffed amaranth and serve immediately.

# Immune-Boosting Turmeric Lassi

Even if we learned to drink lassi (a fresh yoghurt-based smoothie) and cook with turmeric on our trips in India, the whole idea of actually combining those two into a drink was pretty much our own. We were looking for a refreshing drink that could also help to boost our immune system after a long and dark winter, so we added ginger, honey and turmeric to a traditional banana lassi. The result was a wonderful-tasting lassi with an interesting twist in flavour and colour. Turmeric is a strong antioxidant and has been used in traditional Ayurvedic medicine throughout history. Considered to be a spice that cleanses the whole body, especially the liver, it is used to support digestion, and to treat fever, infections and inflammations. The addition of black pepper enhances the anti-inflammatory effect of the turmeric.

When we posted this recipe on our blog, it became something of a viral success and in the following weeks, turmeric lassi popped up on blogs and instagram accounts all over the internet. It even made it onto a few Indian recipe sites.

*450 ml (15 fl oz/2 cups) plain yoghurt with live
   and active live cultures*
*2 ripe bananas*
*2 tsp freshly grated ginger or ground ginger*
*2 tsp clear honey (preferably unheated)*
*juice of ½ lemon*
*2 tsp rosehip powder (optional but delicious
   and a good C-vitamin boost)*
*1 tsp vanilla extract or ground vanilla*
*3–4 tsp ground turmeric (or freshly grated
   turmeric root)*
*a tiny pinch black pepper*
*4–5 ice cubes*

Place all the ingredients in a blender and mix on high speed until smooth. Taste and add more yoghurt if you prefer. Pour the lassi into 2 large or 4 small glasses. For a more stunning presentation, dust with ground turmeric on top before serving. Add a straw and serve.

# Vietnamese Iced Coffee

I tried *ca phe sua da* at several cafés and coffee bars in Ho Cho Minh City and have also begun making it at home on the hottest of summer days or for moments when I need a special pick-me-up. This cold, sweet and yet potently strong drink tastes like a foreign relative of the frappucino. In Vietnam they use a special drip-filter to brew the coffee, but any strong coffee – even a double shot of espresso – works fine. The tradition is to use condensed milk, but here we have whizzed together a date milk as a good plant-based alternative. It has the right thick consistency and sweet flavour. A pinch of cardamom is added for an extra twist. I brew the coffee ahead and let it cool a bit before adding it to the ice. It's not the traditional way of doing it, but helps if you want to drink it without too much melted ice.

I haven't got into beans, grinds and grams here – I simply recommend choosing a coffee that you like. Be aware that it will taste a little different cold – more intense. Balance it with as much sweetened milk as you like. — *David*

*60 ml (2 fl oz/¼ cup) strong, dark filter coffee (preferably Vietnamese) or a double shot of espresso*
*120 ml (4 fl oz/1 cup) unsweetend plant milk (we prefer almond milk)*
*6 fresh, soft dates, stoned*
*½ tsp freshly ground cardamom*

Start by brewing the coffee, then leave to cool down a bit. Prepare the date milk by whizzing up the plant milk with dates and cardamom in a high-speed blender. You will get more milk than you need for one coffee, but just store the rest in the fridge (or make more coffee!)

Pour the slightly cooled coffee into a glass filled with ice, then pour in as much date milk as you like. I find a 40:60 ratio of milk to coffee is perfect.

# Dragon Fruit Milkshake

Dragon fruit (pitaya) must be one of the weirdest-looking fruits on the planet. It's hard to describe it, but it looks a bit like a pink-red-green mango cactus. When it is cut open, the flesh is white and studded with tiny black seeds. We first tried dragon fruit in Thailand and soon used it in salads, desserts and drinks. In contrast to its vibrant exterior, the fruit has a very mild and slightly sweet taste somewhat similar to melon. Its mild flavour is especially refreshing in shakes and smoothies. This exotic version of a milkshake became our favourite on the trip. Ideally you need a soft, young, fresh 'drinking' coconut for this, not a hard, brown one. They are available from some supermarkets and Asian stores and also online. If you can't get one, you can just use coconut milk but it won't be quite the same.

*1 dragon fruit*
*1 banana*
*1 young 'drinking' coconut or*
*    a 400 ml (14 fl oz) can coconut milk*
*1 large handful ice cubes*

Peel the dragon fruit and banana, cut them in large pieces and place in a blender. Open the young coconut and pour the water into a measuring jug. Pour 250 ml (8½ fl oz/ 1 cup) of the coconut water over the fruit, then scoop out 125 g (4 oz/½ cup) of the soft coconut meat and add to the blender. Add the ice cubes and blend until smooth. Serve immediately in tall glasses with straws.

# DESSERTS

# Torta di Ricotta e Polenta

Rich, sweet, moist and yet completely free from flour and refined sugar, this Italian lemon and almond cake is a great way to end a meal. It is technically a cheesecake, but has very little in common with the heavy American versions. In Italy, most delis have their own version of ricotta. The most delicious one is made from sheeps' milk – try it in this recipe, if you can find it. We often prepare the cake a day in advance. It makes it even creamier and enhances the flavours.

*100 g (3½ oz /scant ½ cup) organic butter*
*150 ml (5 fl oz /scant ½ cup) clear honey*
  *(preferably unheated)*
*finely grated zest of 3 organic lemons*
*½ tsp ground vanilla powder or vanilla extract*
*4 eggs, separated*
*140 g (5 oz/1¼ cups) almond flour*
  *(or 140 g (5 oz/1¼ cups) almonds, blitzed*
  *into flour)*
*125 g (4½ oz/1 cup) fine, organic GMO-free*
  *polenta*
*250 g (9 oz/generous 1 cup) ricotta*
*45 g (1½ oz/½ cup) flaked (slivered) almonds*

Preheat the oven to 160°C (325°F/Gas 3). Line the base of a 20 cm (8 in) springform tin with baking parchment and set aside.

Place the butter, half of the honey, the lemon zest and vanilla in a bowl and use an electric mixer to beat everything until creamy. Add the egg yolks and continue to beat for a further minute. Add the almond flour, polenta and ricotta and fold everything together.

Whisk the egg whites in a seperate bowl until softly peaking in a separate bowl. Add the remaining honey and continue whisking until peaking again and well blended. Slowly fold the egg whites into the cake mixture.

Turn the mixture into the prepared cake tin and sprinkle the flaked almonds evenly over the top. Bake for 40–50 minutes or until a toothpick inserted in the centre comes out clean. The centre of the cake might look slightly wobbly at first, but it will firm up when the cake cools down. Leave to cool completely before removing it from the tin.

# Indian Cardamom & Sesame Laddu

For many years I didn't know that the lovely, fragrant Indian sweetmeats I had eaten were called laddu, although I knew perfectly well how good they tasted. A friend and I were on a train from Mumbai to northern Rajasthan when we discovered how cheeky yet friendly fellow travellers in India can be. One minute they steal your seat while you are stretching your legs, and two minutes later they offer you a sample of their wife's homemade sweets. It wasn't until several years later when I found them in our local health food store that I recalled the flavour of butter and roasted chickpea (garbanzo) flour and found out their real name. Funny how far you have to travel to try something that you actually have around the corner at home. We have shaped them into squares here, but you could just as well roll them into balls. — *David*

*100 g (3½ oz/scant ½ cup) ghee or organic butter*
*125 g (4½ oz/generous 1 cup) chickpea (garbanzo) flour*
*1 tsp cardamom seeds (removed from the pods), freshly ground*
*40 g (1½ oz/¼ cup) sesame seeds*
*4 tbsp clear honey (preferably unheated)*

Melt the ghee in a saucepan over a medium-low heat. Add the chickpea flour and freshly ground cardamom. Stir frequently to get rid of any lumps and prevent it from burning. Cook gently for 10–12 minutes, then add the sesame seeds and honey. The mixture should now be thick and slightly golden, with an aroma of roasted chickpeas. Simmer it very gently for a further 5 minutes, stirring all the time, then remove it from the heat. If it seems too liquid you might want to add an extra tablespoon of chickpea flour before removing it from the heat.

Turn out the mixture onto baking parchment on a baking tray. Flatten it out slightly and leave to cool for about 10 minutes. Press it into a flat shape, about 1 cm (½ in) deep. Cut it into 5 x 2.5 cm (2 x 1 in) pieces and leave in the fridge to set.

The laddu will keep in an airtight container at room temperature for a few days or for about a week in the fridge.

# Chilled Rice Pudding & Citrus Syrup

The traditional Danish rice pudding that most Danes serve for Christmas is known as risalamande. If you ask us, once a year is not nearly enough, so we think of it as a winter treat that is just as wonderful during spring, summer and autumn. Traditionally, it is made from rice, double cream, sugar and almonds and topped with cherry compôte. Our recipe is not as heavy, but every ounce as creamy and delicious. The rice is slow-cooked in almond milk and served with a delightful sweet orange syrup. When mandarins are in season, they make a sweeter one.

*Rice Pudding*
*150 g (5 oz/⅔ cup) brown round-grain rice*
*250 ml (8½ fl oz/1 cup) water*
*800 ml (27 fl oz/3½ cups) almond milk*
 *or milk of choice*
*a pinch of sea salt*
*125 g (4 oz/¾ cup) blanched almonds,*
 *chopped*

*Citrus Syrup – makes 120 ml (4 fl oz/½ cup)*
*250 ml (8½ fl oz/1 cup) juice and zest from*
 *organic oranges or mandarins (about*
 *2 large oranges)*
*½ tsp cardamom seeds*
*1 tbsp clear honey (preferably unheated)*

Cook the rice in the water in a heavy-based saucepan for 2 minutes, stirring. Add the milk and bring to the boil, then reduce the heat and cook gently, covered, for 25 minutes. Stir often to prevent burning. Add more milk if needed – it should be very creamy. Add salt to taste. Leave to cool completely, then stir in the chopped almonds.

Meanwhile, make the citrus syrup. Place all the ingredients in a small saucepan and bring to the boil. Reduce the heat immediately and simmer gently, uncovered, until reduced by half – about 20 minutes. Taste and add more honey if needed. Strain to remove the cardamom seeds.

Spoon the cold rice into serving glasses and add a spoonful of the citrus syrup. The rice can be stored in the fridge for 3–5 days; the syrup for up to a week.

# Cinnamon Oranges

Several years ago, I spent a week trying different restaurants and spas in Morocco for a magazine I worked for. It wasn't exactly the worst week of my life. At one of the restaurants I was served an amazing seven-course vegetarian lunch. The food was so spectacular that by the time it came to dessert, I had the highest expectations. 'They will probably end it with a bang,' I remember thinking. Surprisingly, all they came out with was a plate with a few slices of orange with sweetened cinnamon sprinkled on top. My first reaction was disappointment but, after having tried it, I realized how brilliant it was to end a big meal with something light and fresh. It was orange season and my dessert was oozing with flavour. This is now something we often serve at home when we want a quick and fresh dessert. Since our imported oranges never seem to have the same taste as the ones I had in Morocco, we have added a quick step to enhance the flavours. — *David*

*5 oranges*
*1 cinnamon stick*
*1 vanilla pod*
*1 tsp whole cloves*

**To Serve**
*2 tsp ground cinnamon*

Cut one of the oranges in half and squeeze the juice into a small saucepan together with the measured water and the spices. Bring it to a low simmer and then remove from the heat and leave to steep and cool for 15 minutes.

Meanwhile, peel the remaining oranges. It's easiest to use a knife if you want to get all the white membrane off. Slice them in 5 mm (¼ in) thin slices and arrange on a large plate or 4 smaller ones. Pour the spiced orange juice over the orange slices. Serve with some extra cinnamon sprinkled on top.

# Almond Butter Blueberry Cookies

Vegan and gluten-free cookie recipes don't grow on trees. At least not good ones. It's difficult to get the right 'cookieness' without using egg and butter, as they are such an essential part of most recipes – so whenever I find homemade vegan cookies in markets and on food stands, I ask for the recipe. The best-tasting vegan cookies I have tried are often made from nut butter, which totally makes up for the lack of egg and butter. I learned that from a vegan bakery in New York. The cookies here use a mix of almond butter and tahini (sesame paste), which gives them a nice texture and a wonderful spectrum of flavours. We have added some blueberries to the batter, as they add a fresh and gooey twist. We have a recipe for nut butter in our first book. It may be worth looking it up if you plan to put these cookies into your weekly routine. — *David*

*150 g (5 oz/1½ cups) rolled oats*
  *(gluten-free, if intolerant)*
*100 g (3½ oz/⅔ cup) buckwheat flour*
*1 tsp bicarbonate of soda (baking soda)*
*1 tsp sea salt*
*90 ml (3 fl oz/⅓ cup) cold-pressed olive oil*
*120 ml (4 fl oz/½ cup) maple syrup*
*250 g (9 oz/1 cup) almond butter*
*90 g (3¼ oz/⅓ cup) tahini (sesame paste)*
*½ tsp ground vanilla or vanilla extract*
*75 g (2½ oz/½ cup) blueberries*

Preheat the oven to 180°C (350°F/Gas 4). Grind the oats into a coarse flour, using a mortar or food processor. Mix with the buckwheat flour, bicarbonate of soda and salt in a large bowl.

Heat the olive oil, maple syrup, almond butter, tahini and vanilla in a small saucepan over a medium heat. Stir until combined. Pour the melted mixture over the flour mixture, add the blueberries and fold everything together until combined. Shape into 2.5 cm (1 in) balls of dough and place a little apart on a baking sheet lined with baking

parchment. Press down on each one gently with the back of a fork. Bake for 10–12 minutes – don't over-bake or they will be dry. Let them cool for a few minutes and transfer to a wire rack to cool.

These cookies are a bit fragile while warm but firm up as they cool down. They will keep in a cookie jar for 1–2 weeks.

Tip: You can replace almond butter with peanut butter, hazelnut (filbert) butter or cashew butter.

# Mexican Paletas

After a bike adventure on an unusually hot day (even for Mexico), the small paleta shop Flor de Michoacan looked like a mirage, too good to be true. A peek into their freezer didn't make it any more real. It was filled with homemade Mexican ice lollies in a rainbow of colours, all naturally flavoured with fruit, nuts and chocolate. When we got back to Sweden, we ordered some paleta moulds (they can be found on Amazon) and started trying our own recipes. It turned out that it is easier than you would think to create colourful and artistic paletas such as these.

We have come up with three different recipes here that definitely look more advanced than they are. All of them are completely vegan and contain only natural ingredients. The Rainbow Smoothie Paletas are made from fresh fruit and berries mixed with coconut milk and a drip of honey and then layered, while the banana and avocado in the Kiwi, Banana & Avocado Paletas make them super-creamy and naturally sweet. Horchata is a Latin rice and almond drink that we have turned into a paleta and decorated with drizzled chocolate.

*Picture overleaf.*

# Rainbow Smoothie Paletas

*150 g (5 oz/1 cup) strawberries, frozen or fresh*
*250 ml (8½ fl oz/1 cup) full-fat coconut milk*
*6 tbsp clear honey (preferably unheated)*
  *or maple syrup*
*1 lemon*
*175 g (6 oz/1 cup) mango, diced, frozen or fresh*
*2 tbsp unsweetened desiccated (shredded) coconut*
*150 g (5 oz/1 cup) blueberries, frozen or fresh*

These paletas are made in 3 batches – one strawberry layer, one mango layer and one blueberry layer. Put the strawberries, a third of the coconut milk, 2 tablespoons of honey and a good squeeze of the lemon in a blender and purée until smooth. Pour into 8 paleta moulds (they should be about a third full) and place in the freezer for about 30 minutes. Rinse the blender, then add the mango, coconut, half the remaining coconut milk, 2 tablespoons of honey and a good squeeze of lemon to it and purée until smooth. Pour onto the strawberry layer in the paleta moulds, leaving the top third space free for the final layer. Place in the freezer to firm up.

Rinse the blender, then add the blueberries, the remaining coconut milk and honey and the last squeeze of juice from the lemon to the blender and purée until smooth. Use to fill up the moulds and insert lolly sticks. Freeze until firm. The paletas will keep in the freezer for about a month.

# Kiwi, Banana & Avocado Paletas

*4 ripe bananas*
*1 avocado, halved, stone and skin removed*
*6 ripe kiwi fruits*
*4 tbsp clear honey (preferably unheated)*
*   or maple syrup*
*120 ml (4 fl oz/½ cup) water*
*juice of ½ lemon*

Peel and roughly chop the bananas and avocado and place in a blender. Peel the kiwi fruit and add 4 of them to the blender. Slice the remaining 2 thinly. Add the honey, water and lemon to the blender and purée until smooth. Pour into 8 paleta moulds, leaving about 1 cm (½ in) unfilled. Place in the freezer for 15 minutes to firm up slightly, then push a kiwi slice down each side of the banana mixture in each mould to decorate – the mixture will then fill the mould. Insert lolly sticks and freeze until firm. The paletas will keep in the freezer for about a month.

# Horchata Paletas

*½ cup brown or other wholegrain rice*
*75 g (2½ oz/½ cup) blanched almonds*
*750 ml (25 fl oz/3 cups) water*
*12 fresh dates, pitted*
*a pinch of sea salt*
*60 g (2 oz ) 70% minimum cacao*
*   dark chocolate*

Rinse the rice in a sieve under cold water. Place the rice and almonds in a large bowl and cover with hot (not boiling) water. Leave to soak for at least 3 hours, preferably overnight. Drain off the soaking water and tip the mixture into a blender (or into a tall jug if you are using a hand blender), add the measured water and run at high speed until smooth. Depending on the quality of your blender it might remain slightly grainy.

Set a fine sieve (or a cheesecloth if you want it completely smooth) over a jug. Strain, pressing on the solids to extract as much as possible of the creamy liquid. Rinse the blender or jug, then pour the horchata milk back into it. Add the dates and salt and blend until smooth. Pour the horchata mixture into the paleta moulds and place in the freezer to firm up for 30 minutes. Insert lolly sticks and freeze until firm.

To serve, melt the chocolate in a bowl over a pan of gently simmering water. Hold each paleta mould under warm water (not hot) until the paleta loosens. Remove from the moulds. Dip a spoon into the melted chocolate and drizzle across the paletas to create a striped chocolate pattern on both sides. Serve immediately. The paletas will stay fresh in the freezer for about a month before coating in the chocolate.

Serves 4–6 / V / GF

# Baked Banana Fritters

Most Southeast Asian countries have their own version of banana fritters. Thai street vendors sell them stuffed in paper bags as a midday snack, and in Vietnam we tried a version where they mashed the bananas and turned them into something similar to ring doughnuts. In South Asia, Sri Lankan banana fritters are often much sweeter, served as a dessert with ice cream and a generous drizzle of coconut treacle (palm syrup) or honey. What they all have in common is that the bananas are dunked in batter and then deep-fried until crispy. Our version is equally tasty but less strenuous for your heart, since we oven-bake the bananas instead of deep-frying them. Serve them hot with a scoop of ice cream or thick yoghurt.

60 g (2 oz/½ cup) rice flour
1 tsp baking powder
45 g (¾ oz/¾ cup) unsweetened desiccated
   (shredded) coconut, plus extra for serving
4 tbsp sesame seeds, plus extra for serving
2 tbsp clear honey (preferably unheated)
2 tbsp cold-pressed coconut or olive oil
4 tbsp almond milk or milk of your choice
1 egg
finely grated zest and juice of 1 lime,
3 ripe bananas

**To Serve**
4–6 scoops ice cream or thick yoghurt

Preheat the oven to 220°C (425°F/Gas 7) and line a baking sheet with baking parchment. Stir together the flour and baking powder in a bowl. Stir in the coconut and sesame seeds. Melt the honey and coconut oil in a small pan over a very low heat. Remove from the heat, add the almond milk, egg and lime and whisk until frothy. Pour the liquid over the dry ingredients and stir until well combined.

Peel the bananas and split them in half lengthwise, then cut each piece in half widthwise, so you get four equal-sized pieces from each banana. Dip them in the batter – you want them to be covered in it but not excessively. Carefully place them on the baking parchment with the cut side up.

Bake for 10–12 minutes or until golden and crisp. Divide among 4 bowls, add a scoop of ice cream or yoghurt and top with sesame seeds or shredded coconut if you wish to.

# Wild Berry Tart

Not all of our journeys require a passport. During the summers, we often travel around in Sweden or Denmark to visit friends and relatives. These few months when fruit and vegetables are in season and berries are hanging heavy on the bushes are truly magical. One of the simplest and most delicious ways to put the bounties of the Nordic summer to good use is to make a tart. The dough here is made from rolled oats and almond flour. You can use whatever berries you find – just be aware that they differ in tartness (for example, red currants have a more tart flavour than raspberries and blueberries), so adjust the sweetener accordingly.

*100 g (3½ oz/1 cup) rolled oats (gluten-free*
*  if intolerant)*
*50 g (2 oz/½ cup) almond flour*
*2 tbsp cornflour (cornstarch) or potato flour*
*a pinch of sea salt*
*½ tsp vanilla extract or ground vanilla*
*40 g (1½ oz/3 tbsp) cold-pressed coconut oil or*
*  softened butter (if not vegan)*
*2 tbsp maple syrup or clear honey*
*  (preferably unheated)*

### Berry Filling
*450 g (1 lb/2½ cups) fresh berries (we use*
*  blueberries, raspberries, gooseberries and*
*  red currants)*
*1–2 tbsp maple syrup or clear honey*
*  (preferably unheated)*
*finely grated zest and juice of ½ lemon*
*  (1 tbsp lemon juice)*
*2 tbsp mint leaves, finely chopped*

### To Serve
*yoghurt, whipped cream, mascarpone*
*  or ice cream (optional)*

Preheat the oven to 180°C (350°F/Gas 4). Combine the oats with the almond flour, cornflour and sea salt in a bowl. Add the vanilla, coconut oil or butter and maple syrup. With your hands, work the dry ingredients towards the centre into the fat and syrup until the mixture forms a dough. Gather it into a ball, wrap in cling film (plastic wrap), then chill for about 30 minutes.

Toss the berries with maple syrup, lemon and mint in a bowl and set aside for a while to let the flavours develop.

Press the dough evenly into a 20 cm (8 in) tart tin. Trim the dough flush with the edge of the pan, or leave the edges uneven for a more rustic look. Prick the base with a fork and pre-bake for about 10 minutes. Remove from the oven, add 2 cups of the berry mixture and spread out evenly. Bake for about 35 minutes or until the crust is golden and the berry filling is bubbly and juicy. Remove from the oven and spread the remaining berries on top. Serve as it is or with a dollop of yoghurt, whipped cream, mascarpone or ice cream.

# Pineapple Pops

As much as we like Thai food, many of their desserts are somewhat frightening to us – gelatine-filled custards, synthetically coloured bright green, pink or yellow and filled with starch and sugar. No, we prefer a more natural and simple kind of sweet treat. Meet the Pineapple Pops! We know it is a bit of a stretch to call raw pineapple a recipe, but we wanted to include this in the book because of the method that we learned from the Thai street vendors. It's a simple way to peel and cut a pineapple into all-natural lollies. They're great on sunny days or at children's birthday parties. You can eat 'as is' or dip the tip in desiccated (shredded) coconut or melted dark chocolate (or both of them for a touch of decadence).

*1 ripe pineapple*
*4 tbsp desiccated (shredded) unsweetend coconut*
*100 g (3½ oz) 70% minimum cacao dark*
  *chocolate (optional)*

Start by cutting a 1 cm/½ in slice off the base of the pineapple using a sharp chef's knife. Don't cut off the green top as it will become the lolly sticks. Stand the pineapple up and, holding the green top, slice the skin off the sides as thinly as possible. You should now see black dots lined up in a spiral all around the pineapple. Cut away the dots horizontally using a small sharp knife at an even angle above and below them so you end up with V-shaped indents twisting all round the pineapple. Use a chef's knife to cut the pineapple in quarters lengthwise right through the green top. If you prefer thinner pops,

you can just divide the quarters in half lengthwise.

If just using coconut, put it in a small bowl and dip the top third of the pineapple in it. Alternatively, break up the chocolate and melt in a bowl over a pan of hot water. Dip the top of the pineapple first in the chocolate and then in the coconut and prop up to allow the chocolate to set before eating.

Tip: If you think the green top is too difficult to hold, cut it off and insert a wooden skewer instead.

# Buckwheat Crêpes with Passion & Mango Syrup

Put on a blindfold and walk out on to the streets of Paris; there is a very good chance that you will collide with a crêpe stand. Actually, on just about any street corner in all French cities you can get a pretty extraordinary crêpe with a savoury filling or a generous drizzle of syrup or chocolate.

These ones made purely with buckwheat flour, have a wonderful earthiness to them. If you have time, prepare the batter an hour ahead and leave it to rest at room temperature – you will get a much better textured result. Served with this gorgeous, sweet, exotic and slightly ginger-zinged passion and mango syrup, it will really make you smack your lips.

### Passion Syrup
6 passion fruit, halved and pulp
   scooped out
4 tbsp maple syrup or clear honey
   (preferably unheated)
90 ml (3 fl oz/⅓ cup) water
1 cm (½ in) piece fresh ginger, peeled
   and grated
1 vanilla pod, split and seeds scraped
   (keep the pod to use another day for
   infusing flavour)
1–2 ripe mangoes, peeled and cut into
   segments

### Pancake Batter
225 g (8 oz/1⅔ cups) buckwheat flour
3 large eggs
450 ml (15 fl oz/2 cups) plant milk such
   as oat or almond
250 ml (8½ fl oz/1 cup) water
1 tbsp melted cold-pressed coconut oil,
   plus extra for frying
a pinch of sea salt

### To Serve
100 g (3½ oz/scant ½ cup) mascarpone
   cheese or Greek-style yoghurt

To make the syrup, place the the pulp into a saucepan. Add the maple syrup or honey, water, ginger and vanilla seeds and cook over medium-low heat, stirring occasionally, until the syrup thickens. If the syrup is too thin, you can let it reduce on the heat for a few minutes more. Add the mango to the syrup and set aside.

To make the pancake batter, beat all the ingredients together in mixing bowl until smooth. To ensure all the lumps are gone, pass the batter through a sieve. Alternatively, put the flour in a bowl. Add the eggs and half the milk and beat until smooth, then gradually mix in the remaining milk and the water. Finally, stir in the oil and salt. Ideally, leave to rest for an hour, if time. Give it a stir afterwards to make sure the flour doesn't end up in the bottom of the bowl.

Heat a 20 cm (8 in) frying pan over a medium-high heat. Add a tiny knob of coconut oil, and when melted, swirl it round the pan then tip out the excess. Add 4–5 tablespoons of the batter. Tilt the pan in circles to swirl the batter round to coat the base of the pan. Fry for about 45 seconds or until the pancake is golden underneath and set on top then flip over and briefly cook the other side. Slide onto a baking sheet and keep warm while you make the remaining pancakes in the same way.

Fold the crêpes into quarters. If liked, return them to the pan and heat through with some of the mango and syrup. Serve the crêpes with a spoonful of the mango and passion syrup and a dollop of mascarpone cheese or yoghurt.

# Double Chocolate Rye Muffins

'We have a surprise for you,' my parents told me. I was 10 years old and had spent my first two days in the USA inside our small hotel room in New York, suffering from a high temperature. From behind her back, my mum pulled out the biggest chocolate muffin I had ever seen. I had only known European muffins before and this was about three times bigger. I threw myself on it and somehow managed to eat the whole thing in no time. I remember lying on my bed with greasy chocolate fingers and a swollen belly, thinking that if all chocolate muffins were like this one, then I definitely had to move to New York City when I was older.

Our muffins are not as big but they are decadent enough to fill your belly, warm your heart, smudge your fingers with chocolate and put a broad smile on your lips. At a quick glance they look like the naughtiest treats in town, but they are actually pretty good for you – our muffins are stuffed with wholegrain rye, coconut milk and natural sweeteners. If you steal one straight from the oven, the bitter, dark chocolate will still be runny on the top ... and you don't have to move to NYC to try it. — *David*

### Dry Ingredients

150 g (5 oz/1 cup) wholegrain rye flour
125 g (4½ oz/scant 1 cup) fine spelt flour
40 g (1½ oz/⅓ cup) raw cacao or unsweetened
   cocoa powder
2 tsp baking powder
1 tsp bicarbonate of soda (baking soda)
1 tsp coarse sea salt
100 g (3½ oz) 70% minimum cacao dark
   chocolate, coarsely chopped

### Wet Ingredients

3 eggs
250 ml (8 ½ fl oz/1 cup) full-fat coconut milk
150 ml (5 fl oz/⅔ cup) maple syrup
150 ml (5 fl oz/⅔ cup) cold-pressed olive oil

Preheat the oven to 200°C (400°F/Gas 6). Line a 12-cup muffin tin with paper cases.

Sift together the dry ingredients except the salt and chocolate in a large mixing bowl. Add half the sea salt and reserve the remainder for topping. Add half the chocolate and set the rest aside.

Beat the eggs in a separate bowl for about a minute. Then add the coconut milk, maple syrup and olive oil while constantly whisking. Add the dry mixture to the wet mixture and use a spatula to carefully fold everything until combined.

Divide the batter among the muffin cases and top with the remaining dark chocolate. Bake for about 18 minutes until well risen and spongey and the chocolate has melted. Remove from the oven and sprinkle with the remaining sea salt. The muffins are best enjoyed still warm from the oven, but they will keep for a week in an airtight container and they freeze well.

Tip: This recipe is a bit heavy on maple syrup, but it is needed to balance the bitterness from the rye and chocolate. You could replace some of it with a ripe banana or pear for a healthier and fruitier touch.

# Quick Airplane Lemon Bars

We make sure we prepare a snack bag when we fly somewhere and these bars seem to always end up in the bag. They are great to have as a pick-me-up when blood sugar or mood is starting to get low, but we also love them because they are made from only four ingredients, take literally five minutes to prepare and have a very sweet yet fresh taste. We usually prepare them the night before we travel and leave them in the fridge overnight to firm up. Wrapped in some baking parchment, they can be kept in a handbag. As always with these basic recipes, you can replace ingredients with what you have at home. Lemon juice can be substituted for apple juice, cashew nuts for almonds, or use sunflower seeds if you're aiming for a nut-free version. If you don't have fresh dates, soak dried dates first and drain and dry them before using.

*150 g (5 oz/1 cup) raw cashew nuts*
*15 soft fresh dates, pitted*
*50 g (2 oz/½ cup) unsweetened desiccated*
  *(shredded) coconut*
*60 ml (2 fl oz/¼ cup) lemon juice*

Place the cashew nuts in a food processor and run it for about 20 seconds to chop them into a coarse 'flour'. Transfer to a bowl and add the dates, coconut and lemon juice to the food processor. Run until it's a sticky mixture. Transfer the mixture to the nut flour and work everything into a thick, slightly sticky dough. Press the dough firmly into a small rectangle, about 10 cm (4 in) long, 15 cm (6 in) wide and 1 cm (½ in) thick. Leave in the fridge for at least an hour or overnight and then cut out six 2.5cm (1 in) wide bars.

Wrap them in baking parchment and store in the fridge. They will keep for at least 24 hours in a warm handbag and for weeks in the fridge.

Tip: You can also use dried dates if you soak them an hour ahead to make them softer.

# Roasted Strawberry & Pine Nut FroYo

I met Luise in Rome, and one of my favourite things about it is that we got to take part in the long and sacred Italian tradition of dating at a gelato bar. The most romantic couples share a cone so that their noses accidentally touch when they are eating. I was too much of an ice-cream addict to settle for half a portion and instead took a three-flavour high ice-cream tower. Fortunately we became a couple anyway and soon my deep love for ice cream had been replaced by a deeper love for Luise. I still love a good ice cream on a warm night, but now I have learned to share. When we make ice cream at home, we like to make it yoghurt-based (FroYo). Roasting the strawberries gives them a sweeter and slightly fruitier flavour. They are wonderful paired with the sweet, creamy pine nuts (pine kernels) and tangy Greek yoghurt. Serve in cones or in bowls, sprinkled with extra pine nuts. Italian makers of ice cream always point out the importance of using good-quality fruit, so look for the ripest and most lipstick-red strawberries at the market. — *David*

*500 g (1 lb 2 oz/generous 3 cups) strawberries*
*120 ml (4 fl oz/½ cup) maple syrup*
*1 tbsp lemon juice*
*½ tsp vanilla extract or 1 vanilla pod, seeds*
  *scraped*
*2 cups full-fat Greek-style or Turkish yoghurt*
  *(for vegans, use GMO-free soya yoghurt)*
*40 g (1½ oz/¼ cup) pine nuts (pine kernels),*
  *finely chopped*

Preheat the oven to 180°C (350°F/Gas 4) and line a baking sheet or large baking dish with baking parchment.

Hull the strawberries, then rinse and drain them. Cut each strawberry in half or quarters, depending on their size. Place in a bowl with 2 tablespoons of the maple syrup, the lemon juice and the vanilla extract or seeds. Toss until all the berries are covered in syrup, then spread out in a single layer on the baking sheet. Roast for 30–40 minutes. The berries should have shrunk in size and released a syrupy juice. Take the baking sheet from the oven, scrape the berries and juice into a small bowl, mash lightly with a fork and as soon as they are cold place them in the fridge.

Meanwhile, stir together the yoghurt, pine nuts and the remaining maple syrup in a bowl. Leave the bowl in the fridge until the strawberries are chilled.

Pour the yoghurt mixture and half of the strawberries into an ice-cream maker and freeze according to the manufacturer's instructions. When the ice cream is almost done, add the remaining strawberries and let the machine run for another minute. Transfer the mixture into a freezerproof container and freeze until firm.

Alternatively, mix together the yoghurt and strawberries and put in a freezerproof shallow container. Place in the freezer and leave for about an hour until frozen round the edges. Whisk with a fork to break up any frozen sections. Return to the freezer and freeze until firm, about 2 hours, whisking with a fork every 30 minutes to break up the ice crystals. Cover and leave in the freezer until ready to serve.

Tip: You can also make this FroYo with thawed frozen strawberries – just skip roasting them and bump up the maple syrup a bit.

# No-flour Chocolate Cake

There are numerous stories floating around the internet on how the no-flour chocolate cake was invented. Many of them say that it was an unintentional mistake by a baker during the 1920s. Apparently he forgot to add the flour to an almond cake that he baked for a party. If it is true, it might be one of the most delicious mistakes of the century. We have tried various no-flour cakes and tortes in France and southern Europe and they are always spectacularly good. Most of the cakes use a base of ground nuts, dried fruit and eggs, which makes them moist, sweet and slightly crunchy. Our chocolate cake is quite classic, but with a Moroccan twist. Dates are the only sweetener, orange is added for the flavour and pomegranate seeds are sprinkled on top. The cake is perfectly moist and deeply decadent from the dark chocolate, cacao powder and ground hazelnuts (filberts). It's a very popular cake in our family and we make it for all kind of holiday parties and birthday celebrations.

300 g (10½ oz/generous 2 cups) raw hazelnuts
  (filberts) or nuts of choice
25 fresh soft dates (about 350 g/12 oz/2 cups)
  or soaked dried dates, stoned and
  roughly chopped
5 eggs, separated
finely grated zest and juice of 1 orange
3 tbsp raw cacao or unsweetened cocoa powder
½ tsp bicarbonate of soda (baking soda)
75 g (2½ oz/⅓ cup) butter
200 g (7 oz) 70% minimum cacao
  dark chocolate

**To Serve**
450 ml (15 fl oz/2 cups) whipped cream
  or thick yoghurt
100 g (3½ oz/¾ cup) pomegranate seeds
  or fresh berries

Preheat the oven to 180°C (350°F/Gas 4). Line a 20 cm (8in) springform cake tin with baking parchment.

Place the nuts in a food processor and pulse until you have a fine-textured flour. Tip into a small bowl and set aside. Add the dates, egg yolks, orange zest and juice, cacao and bicarbonate of soda to the food processor and run at high speed until it has become a sticky mixture. Transfer it to a large mixing bowl.

Melt the butter and 150 g (5 oz) of the dark chocolate in a bowl over a pan of hot water and pour it into the date mixture together with the ground hazelnuts. Stir until well combined. Use an electric mixer to whisk the egg whites until soft peaks have formed, then fold them into the rest of the batter. Pour the batter into the prepared cake tin and bake for about 1 hour 10 minutes, or until the cake is firm but not dry. Remove from the oven and leave until cold before taking it out of the cake tin.

Spread the cake with whipped cream on top, or serve it with some yoghurt on the side. Shave the remaining chocolate over it and finish off with a large handful of pomegranate seeds or fresh berries. Serve immediately. The cake will keep in the fridge for 3–5 days.

DESSERTS

# Raw Key Lime Mousse

Although Key Lime Pie is a classic American dessert, we came up with this raw Key Lime-inspired recipe in Morocco. All the ingredients were right in front of us one morning at the market so it was simple for us to mix them all together into an ultra-creamy, sweet and tangy mousse. This would be a good dessert to serve at a non-formal party or brunch, as it's very easy and quick to prepare any number of them a few hours ahead and then chill them in the fridge.

*2 ripe avocados*
*finely grated zest and juice of 2 limes*
*6 fresh soft dates, stoned (or dried dates, soaked*
  *for 20 minutes in warm water, then drained)*
*1 pomegranate, seeds scooped out and separated*

Cut the avocados in half. Remove the stone, use a spoon to scoop out the avocado flesh into a bowl and discard the skin and stones. Add the lime zest and juice and the dates. Use a hand blender to process until completely smooth, or blend all the ingredients in a food processor. Taste and add more lime or dates if needed.

Spoon the mixture into 4 small serving glasses and chill for a few hours to firm slightly. Serve with a generous amount of pomegranate seeds piled on top. The mixture can be stored for a couple of days in the fridge in an airtight container then spooned into glasses just before serving.

# CONDIMENTS

# Raw Raspberry & Chia Jam

Even though it can sometimes be very fulfilling to slow-cook a traditional jam made from ripened fresh fruit, we often realize that we need a jar of jam at very short notice when fruit isn't in season. Instead of taking a trip to the store, we simply reach into our freezer for some frozen berries and mix them with a little syrup and chia seeds – no sugar or heating needed. After only ten minutes, the chia seeds have transformed the berries into a jam-like consistency. Use as you would a normal jam – on top of pancakes, waffles, sandwiches and scones.

*250 g (9 oz/2 cups) fresh or thawed*
*   *frozen raspberries*
*2 tbsp chia seeds*
*2 tsp maple syrup or clear honey*
*   (preferably unheated)*

Place the berries in a bowl and mash with a fork. Stir in the chia seeds and maple syrup. Whisk to combine, then set aside for 10 minutes, stirring every now and then to prevent the chia seeds from sticking together. Store in an airtight glass jar in the fridge for up to 5 days.

# Pico de Gallo Spread

In our kitchen, the classic Mexican salsa pico de gallo is turned into a creamy spread. We oven-roast tomatoes and (bell) peppers to increase their sweeter tones. It balances the sting from the chilli, coriander (cilantro) and onion perfectly. Use it in our Lentil & Strawberry Tacos on page 69 or with the Mexican Breakfast Salad on page 48.

*4 tomatoes, halved*
*2 red (bell) peppers, halved and seeded*
*½ onion, diced*
*½ green jalapeño chilli, seeded and*
*    finely chopped*
*1 small handful coriander (cilantro),*
*    chopped*
*juice of ½ lime*

Preheat the oven to 200°C (400°F/Gas 6). Place the tomatoes and peppers on a baking tray, cut side down. Roast for about 30 minutes or until slightly charred. Remove from the oven and leave to cool slightly. When cool enough to handle, peel off the skins and place the tomatoes and peppers in a food processor or blender. Pulse a few times, aiming for a chunky-smooth consistency.

Pour into a bowl, add the remaining ingredients and stir to combine. Taste and adjust the flavours if needed. The spread will keep in an airtight glass jar in the fridge for a couple of weeks.

CONDIMENTS

# Cacao & Hazelnut Spread

This is our version of Nutella – it's less sweet and has an intense and wholesome flavour. Use it on top of rye bread, on your morning smoothie bowl or inside the Rye & Chocolate Croissants on page 53.

You can substitute cold-pressed coconut oil for the cacao butter – the taste will be different but delicious too.

*375 g (13 oz/3 cups) raw hazelnuts (filberts)
or nuts of your choice
125 g (4 oz/½ cup) cacao butter
(or cold-pressed coconut oil, the taste will be
different but delicious too)
20 fresh dates or soaked dried dates, stoned
4 tbsp raw cacao or unsweetened cocoa powder
120 ml (4 fl oz/½ cup) water or more if
you prefer*

Preheat the oven to 150°C (300°F/Gas 2). Place the nuts in a single layer on a baking sheet. Toast in the oven for about 20 minutes until they are golden and the skins are starting to split – keep an eye on them to prevent them from burning. Remove from the oven and leave to cool slightly. Place the nuts on a rough-textured, clean tea towel (dishcloth) and rub to remove the skins, then place them in a food processor and process until completely smooth (like nut butter) and their oil has been released. You may want to scrape down the sides of the food processor a couple of times.

Melt the cacao butter or coconut oil in a small saucepan over a very low heat. Mash the dates with a fork until they have the consistency of sticky caramel. Add the melted cacao butter, cacao powder, mashed dates and water to the nut butter and process until smooth. Alternatively, combine the mixture by stirring with a spoon. Thin with a little more water, if preferred. Taste and add more cacao powder, if preferred.

Spoon into airtight glass jars and store in the fridge. It will keep for several weeks.

Tip: Add the finely grated zest and juice of an orange instead of some of the water for an extra twist.

# Za'atar Spice Blend

At first we kept this Middle Eastern and North African spice blend in our spice cabinet, but it quickly advanced up the ranks and got placed right next to the salt on our kitchen counter. We use it on roasted vegetables, in salads, on hummus or on soft-boiled eggs, but it can really be used on almost anything savoury. It adds a salty yet tangy twist. Add 1 tablespoon of ground cumin for really nice optional addition.

*4 tbsp sesame seeds*
*4 tbsp ground sumac*
*2 tbsp dried thyme*
*2 tbsp oregano*
*1 pinch of sea salt*

Place the sesame seeds in a frying pan and gently toast over a low heat, stirring until lightly toasted (or you can use them raw). Remove from the heat and tip into a bowl immediately to prevent over-browning. Leave to cool then combine with the remaining ingredients. Transfer to an airtight glass jar. This spice blend will keep for months in a dark cupboard.

# Dried Plum Sauce

This is a wonderfully simple version of an Asian sweet and sour sauce that we use for dipping steamed vegetables or dumplings in. See the Mushroom & Tofu Dumplings recipe on page 165.

*225 g (8 oz/1 cup) dried plums, pitted*
*120 ml (4 fl oz/½ cup) water*
*2 tbsp lemon juice, or more to taste*
*2 tbsp clear honey (preferably unheated)*

Place all the ingredients in a blender and mix until smooth. Add more water or lemon juice if needed. Store in a screw-topped jar in the fridge. It will keep for several weeks.

# Mango & Raisin Chutney

This well-flavoured chutney has a nice balance between sweet and tangy. We eat it with the Masala Dosa on page 83 and the Whole Egg Flower Curry on page 161, but don't just limit it to Indian food as it adds a nice kick to almost any savoury dish.

*Spice bundle*
*1 cinnamon stick*
*2 cloves*
*2 cardamom pods*
*1 tsp cumin seeds*
*1 tsp coriander seeds*
*1 tsp grated fresh ginger*

*Chutney*
*1 ripe mango*
*1 small handful raisins*
*175 ml (6 fl oz/¾ cup) water*
*4 tbsp apple cider vinegar*
*½ tsp dried chilli flakes or more to taste*
*2 tbsp clear honey (preferably unheated)*
  *or maple syrup*
*½ tsp sea salt*

Place all the spices in a tea bag or tie up in a piece of cheesecloth. Peel the mango, cut off all the flesh and discard the stone. Place the spice bundle, mango flesh, raisins and water in a saucepan and bring to the boil over a medium heat. Reduce the heat and simmer gently for 10 minutes, stirring occasionally.

Add the vinegar, chilli, honey and salt, cover and continue to simmer for 30 minutes until thick and pulpy. Taste and add more vinegar, honey or salt if needed. Leave to cool completely then transfer to an airtight container. It will keep in the fridge for a couple of weeks.

# Index

# About the Authors

David Frenkiel and Luise Vindahl are the couple behind the award-winning vegetarian food blog Green Kitchen Stories, which has followers from all over the world. Healthy, seasonal and delicious vegetarian recipes paired with colourful and beautiful photographs have become the trademark of their style. This is their second cookery book. The first, *The Green Kitchen* (UK) / *Vegetarian Everyday* (US), has been published in eight countries and is highly acclaimed.

David and Luise's work has appeared in *Food & Wine Magazine, Bon Appetit, ELLE, Vogue, The Guardian, Vegetarian Times* and many more publications. In 2013 their blog won the Best Food Blog Awards hosted by *Saveur Magazine*. They have released two best-selling apps for iPhone and iPad which have been selected in App Store Best of 2012 and 2013.

Luise is Danish and David is Swedish. They currently live in Stockholm with their daughter Elsa. Apart from doing freelance recipe development and food photography, David works as a freelance graphic designer and Luise is a qualified nutritional therapist.

Read more on *www.greenkitchenstories.com*

# Thank You

Thank you!

To our awesome blog readers. You are the very reason that we have dared pursuing our dreams and started writing books. All your feedback, cheering comments and many questions help us improve our way of cooking everyday.

To our beloved families, both in Denmark and Sweden, for following us on our trips, loaning your car to us, playing with Elsa while we work and encouraging us in whatever steps we choose to take. We love you and your support means the world to us.

To all of you kind people who have opened up your homes and couches for us in various house swaps, loans and AirBnB rentals. We are so grateful for the opportunity to spend our travelling days in real homes instead of hotel rooms and motels. You are welcome to our home anytime you visit Stockholm.

To Fouzia, Jazmine and all other mothers and home chefs that have invited us into your kitchens around the world and taught us how to cook genuine local food.

To Kate, Kajal, Stephen and the rest of the gang at Hardie Grant, for believing in a book that captures two of our greatest passions – food and travels.

To Carolyn, for finding all the small glitches and irregularities in the recipes. And for making our English sound better than it actually is.

To Charlotte for designing another beautiful book for us.

To Elsa, for being you.

GREEN KITCHEN TRAVELS

First published in 2014 by Hardie Grant Books

Hardie Grant Books (UK)
Dudley House, North Suite
34–35 Southampton Street
London WC2E 7HF
www.hardiegrant.co.uk

Hardie Grant Books (Australia)
Ground Floor, Building 1
658 Church Street
Melbourne, VIC 3121
www.hardiegrant.com.au

British Library Cataloguing-in-Publication Data. A catalogue record
for this book is available from the British Library.

ISBN: 978-174270-768-6

Publisher: Kate Pollard
Desk Editor: Kajal Mistry
Copy and Recipe Editor: Carolyn Humphries
Proofreader: Diana Vowles
Indexer: Cathy Heath
Internal and Cover Design: Charlotte Heal
Design Assistant: Katherine Jenkins
Photography © David Frenkiel
Colour Reproduction by P2D

Find this book on Cooked.
Cooked.com.au
Cooked.co.uk

Printed and bound in China by 1010
10 9 8 7 6 5 4 3 2 1